Georgina M. Synge

**A Ride Through Wonderland**

Georgina M. Synge

**A Ride Through Wonderland**

ISBN/EAN: 9783744759632

Printed in Europe, USA, Canada, Australia, Japan

Cover: Foto ©Andreas Hilbeck / pixelio.de

More available books at **www.hansebooks.com**

# THE YELLOWSTONE NATIONAL PARK

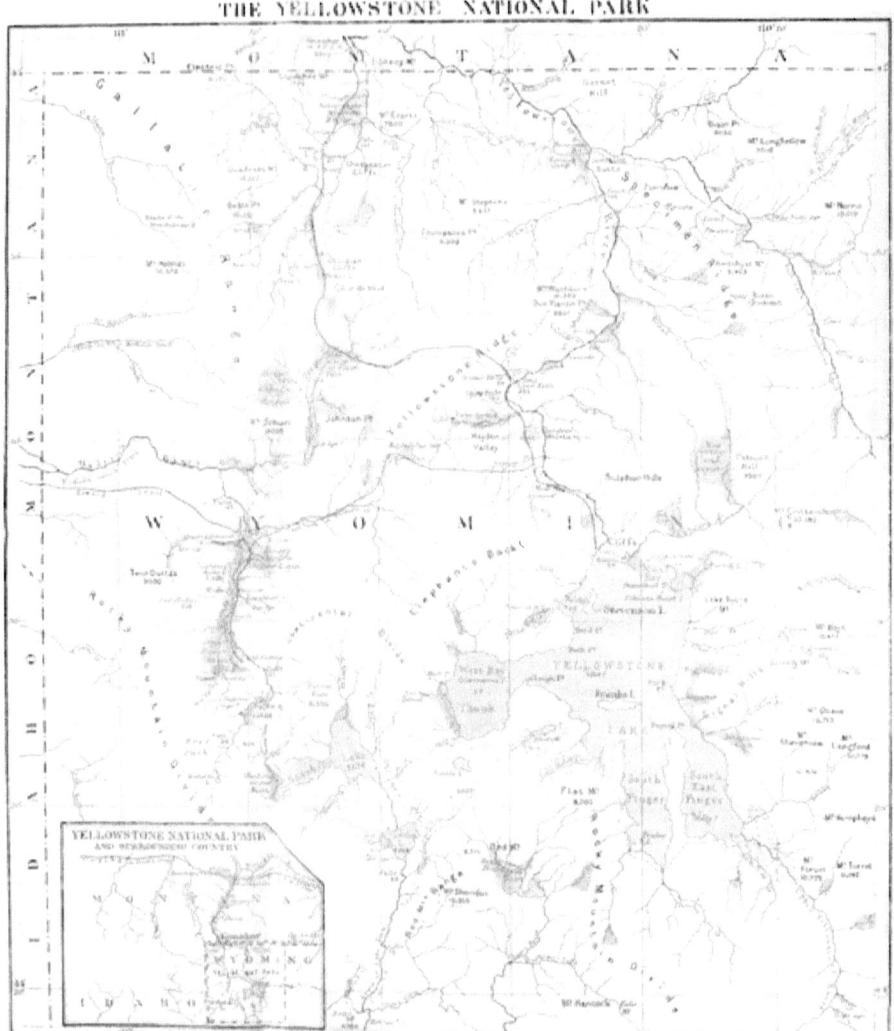

# A RIDE THROUGH WONDERLAND

BY

GEORGINA M. SYNGE

AUTHOR OF "GREAT-GRANDMAMMA," ETC.

*WITH TWO ILLUSTRATIONS*

LONDON
SAMPSON LOW, MARSTON & COMPANY
*Limited*
St. Dunstan's House
FETTER LANE, FLEET STREET, E.C.
1892

# CONTENTS.

### CHAPTER I.
|  | PAGE |
|---|---|
| THE FIRST HUNDRED MILES | 1 |

### CHAPTER II.
| A HURRICANE | 25 |

### CHAPTER III.
| THE GREAT DIVIDE AND FIREHOLE BASIN | 31 |

### CHAPTER IV.
| GEYSER-LAND | 49 |

### CHAPTER V.
| BIG GAME | 71 |

### CHAPTER VI.
| YELLOWSTONE LAKE | 85 |

### CHAPTER VII.
| THE GREAT CAÑON AND FALLS | 91 |

## CONTENTS.

### CHAPTER VIII.
A Digression on "Holding Up" . . . 102

### CHAPTER IX.
Norris Basin . . . . . . 111

### CHAPTER X.
Mammoth Hot Springs . . . . 119

### CHAPTER XI.
Lost in the Yellowstone . . . 138

---

# ILLUSTRATIONS.

The Fall of the Yellowstone . . . 93
The Mammoth Springs . . . . 125

# A RIDE THROUGH WONDERLAND.

## CHAPTER I.

### THE FIRST HUNDRED MILES.

For so the Yellowstone Park may well be called.

Though why " Park " it is difficult to say, as an area of about 3570 square miles is not usually described by that name. However, it seems to be an elastic term in America. " Keep off the Park," we noticed written up on a post in conspicuous letters near a tiny square of well-watered grass, about the size of a drawing-room carpet, which constituted the sole adornment of a little barren wayside town of wooden shanties.

It is a great thing on visiting a place to

be able to say, like the Queen of Sheba, that the half has not been told us.

Although we had read thrilling and fascinating accounts of this marvellous region, yet each day we had to confess that it far surpassed our most fervent imaginings. Perhaps, however, those who go through in the ordinary mode by stage, herded along on their "forty dollar tickets" in five days, and missing half its beauty and wonders, may not be so enthusiastic. For the only way to thoroughly appreciate and enjoy it is to give oneself plenty of time, and to ride or drive through quite independently.

The Yellowstone Park lies chiefly in the north-western part of Wyoming, though it contains also a small strip of Montana and Idaho. On its western side lie the broken ranges of the Rocky Mountains, and to the south of it runs the great Continental Divide. The altitude is very great. Even the lowest valleys are 6000 feet above the sea, some of them being a good deal higher, while several of the mountain peaks are 10,000 to 12,000 feet. As the nights are seldom free from frost, farming is out of the question, and, owing to its volcanic nature, the land has little mercantile value. But for surpassing wonders and beauties, for interests varied and unceasing at almost every step of the way, it must stand as one of the most favoured spots on the earth, and one feels what a wise act it was of the U.S. Congress (in 1872) to make of it a National Reservation, devoted to the enjoyment of all people.

For here are found geysers excelling those of Iceland or any yet discovered; hot pools of every rainbow hue; springs for ever bubbling forth their sulphur, iron, or alum streams; cañons into whose black depths no human foot has penetrated; falls higher than any in the world of the same volume; forests full of antelope, elk, and bear; rivers teeming with trout. A programme indeed of entrancing delights, and at present unspoilt, and, except along the beaten track, untouched by man!

We made sundry inquiries before we

set out on our tour as to the best end by which to reach the Park. Nearly everyone advised us to take the Mammoth Springs entrance, as the Northern Pacific Railway runs a branch line to Cinnabar, only six miles distant. As, however, we intended coming up from Salt Lake by the Utah Northern, we decided to enter the other end from Beavor Cañon, which, although 115 miles from the Park, is the nearest point the railway touches. This route leads through a delightfully wild and unfrequented country, abounding most of the way with game, and for those who can spare the time it is well worth the extra journey.

We procured the greater part of our stores at Salt Lake, laying in enough to last ourselves and two men for about a fortnight. We made our purchases at the Mormon Co-operative Stores, and found all our "saintly" food most satisfactory. We were served by a modest young Mormon, who told us he had been employed in the Army and Navy Stores in London before he became a saint, but found the Mormon hours, and holidays, and pay, more satisfactory; also doubtless the choice of wives, though he did not mention this.

Beavor Cañon is the funniest little place. As we had to wait there three days to collect our outfit (and scour the country for a side-saddle, an article which we had foolishly omitted to bring), we had plenty of time for observation. It stands between two low ridges of hills which form the entrance to the Cañon, and consists of several rows of little wooden houses and a few rather larger ones "dumped" here and there on its brown treeless level. Enormous signboards announced that a large percentage of these mansions were "restaurants" and "beer saloons." The hotel is decidedly primitive, and as the air does not seem to suit either cows or hens, the luxuries produced by these useful species come from a distance, and are rather scarce. The railway runs through the middle of the town, and, as there is no road (and only one or two trains in the day), forms the fashionable resort of the inhabitants on Sundays and fine evenings. One great drawback to enjoying this, however, is that one's eyes have to be more or less glued to one's footsteps, as the sleepers are raised rather high above the ground, and a glance upwards may land one upon one's nose.

The day before we started, our horses were brought round for us to try. As my side-saddle had not arrived, and having terrible stories of bucking "cayuses" in my mind, I must confess I felt some trepidation on mounting my wiry-looking little beast, and having to sit helplessly sideways on the big Mexican saddle. However, "Bolly" turned out of most lamb-like demeanour, and I "loped"[1] him up and down under the critical eyes of a group of cowboys who were sitting on some wooden doorsteps, chewing straws, and surveying us with rather disdainful glances.

A.'s horse, "Snip," was more of an Eastern build than the others, which were cayuses (a cross between the American

---

[1] The American word for canter.

horse and the mustang). He was rounder in the barrel, and much less weedy-looking, and though not quite so sure-footed, was a very good goer. The guide rode a big raw-boned beast of wonderful enduring powers, but which bucked steadily for five minutes each time he was mounted, a considerable drawback in our unaccustomed eyes. Then there were two stout animals, a roan and a grey, to draw the waggon, a vehicle on half springs covered with canvas, something like a grocer's cart.

We got all our outfit together at last, Messrs. Bassett Bros., who run the stages through the Park Reservation, supplying us at about seventeen dollars per day. This included the hire and forage of the horses, a guide, a lad to drive the waggon, a tent, and cooking utensils, etc.

A. was for taking no mattress—"roll yourself up in a rug, and there you are," was his idea. But as I ventured to differ as to the delights of this method, we ended by procuring huge bags filled with fresh hay, which were most comfortable.

We also took about eight blankets and a mackintosh cover. A small leather portmanteau contained our changes of raiment and toilet necessaries, also such useful things as tools, fishing gear, and a few simple ointments and medicines. My costume was peculiar, as it had to be adapted to walking and climbing as well as horseback. It consisted of riding trousers and high leather leggings, a very short tweed skirt, a crimson flannel blouse, and a cowboy's felt hat to keep off the sun. We each wore a leather belt with pockets, containing collapsible drinking cups, compasses, knives and string, etc., which we found a great comfort.

As for our food, we took a good load of tinned beef and tongue, sardines, flour, biscuits, bacon, coffee, cracked wheat, tinned milk and fruit, and a bottle of Worcester sauce (without which no American table is complete); also two bottles of whiskey and a box of Mormon beer, "in case," as A. remarked, "the water might be injurious."

We started on the 1st of September—a glorious day. A brilliant sun and crisp fresh air, every breath of which felt like a tonic. We set forth early in the morning, as we had about thirty miles to ride before reaching a good camping ground. This first thirty miles is the least interesting part of the way, though its wide undulating sweeps covered thickly with sage-brush, with here and there a solitary group of pine or aspen standing bleak against the sky, have a fascination of their own, and seemed to us a fitting entrance to the weird and wonderful land beyond.

All among this sage-brush on each side of us were innumerable badger holes, terrible to behold; and though A. and Snip made frequent short cuts, I, having a distinct aversion to breaking my neck needlessly, kept steadily to the trail. It is wonderful, though, how knowing the Western horses are in avoiding these dangerous pitfalls. Bolly always seemed to keep a sharp look out, and would give an indignant little snuff of disapprobation on passing near one; and as he never by any chance put his foot into them, I grew quite resigned to even " loping " over them at last.

Beesley, the guide, was inclined to be rather morose and taciturn, but Jim, the lad who drove the waggon, was quite the reverse, and told us all his family history as he cooked our lunch. He informed us he always liked " doin' the thing " with English folk; they weren't mean like the Yanks, who grudged you every bite you took. After this pleasing eulogy, of course, I hadn't a word to say on discovering that a little basket of pears, brought for my special refection, and placed in a corner of the waggon, was nearly empty!

How delicious that first meal was, free from all the humdrum conventionalities of life, surrounded by wild stretches of country, with not a human habitation or sign of human life visible.

Our bread was baked in a small cast-iron Dutch-oven, something like a gipsy's kettle, the edges of the cover being turned up to hold the hot embers; I never tasted bread more excellent. In this oven, too, we could cook our meat or fish. The men always ate with us, quite at home and at their ease, as we sat together on the waggon seats round our little camp table. For when you come Far West every man is as good as another, and everybody you meet is a "gentleman," whether it is the boy who blacks your boots or the rich man who owns his millions. I must say we found them most well-mannered and agreeable (with the exception of Beesley, whom we afterwards changed), and most eager that we should see everything we could.

My horse seemed to me very rough at first, and the saddle not all that might be desired, with its sharp little pummels and generally antiquated structure; but I soon became accustomed to both, and Bolly's steady "lope," kept up mile after mile as if he were propelled by clockwork, was really much less fatiguing for long distances than the uncertain paces of an Eastern horse. In these regions, too, horses are all bitted with a single rein on a very sharp curb, so that the merest touch is sufficient to control them. Indeed, the reins seem very little used, and are often left hanging quite loose, all the guiding being done by knee pressure.

We reached our first camping ground, in the Camas Meadows—brown grass-covered levels surrounded by mountains—by about five o'clock in the afternoon. We chose a snug spot on the lee of a small hill covered with clumps of fir and close to a dear little icy-cold spring, which bubbled out of the earth, edged with a winding green fringe of grass to mark its course along the burnt-up ground.

What fun it was pitching our tent for the first time, and gathering wood for a huge camp fire, and picketing the horses, and exploring our surroundings, and discovering a little forsaken "dug-out" on the hill-side, a sort of hole scooped in the earth, and roofed with branches, the temporary home of some prospector or pioneer.

We slept like tops, nor did we feel the least cold, though our sponges were frozen hard the next morning. We were awakened by a little chip-munk, a sort of tiny squirrel (not much larger than a mouse), that jumped about on the top of our tent uttering shrill little cries. Nearly everywhere we stopped we had these curious little creatures peeping in and out amongst our things, moved evidently with a violent curiosity, and quite untroubled by fears. They would come close up to us and would eat crumbs almost out of our hands, and they always were to be seen scampering about the horses' feet when they were having their corn, and would sit up so prettily, with their furry tails over their backs, and munch the scattered grains.

We started soon after breakfast on the second day, leaving the men to pack up and follow with the waggon. Gradually our surroundings were becoming more broken and hilly. Fresh ranges of mountains began to loom up on all sides, sometimes so clearly defined, their lights and shadows so distinct, that they appeared but a few miles off.

There is no blue like the blue of the

Rockies, there are no colours of so subtle and varying hues. Sometimes they appear like distant fading spirits, then suddenly they seem to stand out like splashes of pure cobalt, relieved only by the black shadows where the cañons cut their way, or the tall dark pine are massed along their base. Every step discloses more wild and lovely vistas, far-away grassy stretches, rugged gorges, dark and mysterious forests, always enclosed peak behind peak by that lovely, dreamy blue. A wonderful silence seems to reign. Birds are rare, there is little buzz of insect life. The wild beasts keep out of sight, as a rule, and do not raise their voices by day. Everything seems wrapped in an unbroken calm. Within ourselves an exhilaration of delight, a capacity for enjoyment rarely equalled; we felt indeed as if nothing could every weary us in that glorious air!

Every now and then we crossed a little creek, a tributary of the Great Snake River, the magnificent falls of which we had seen a few days before at Shoshone.

Some of these had very suggestive names. Bottle Creek, we were told, was so called because Generals Sherman and Sheridan once camped there and left behind them such a surprising number of bottles. Shot.Gun Creek, too, seems to speak for itself. We passed a log cabin near the latter where lives a trapper of renown. Elk antlers were suspended over the doorway and ornamented the four corners of the roof, while skins of bear and other beasts were stretched on every available piece of wall.

It was late in the evening when we caught a glimpse of the Snake River itself, silently hurrying, white and gleaming, through dark forest-covered banks to its awful distant leap. We splashed through its shallow bed, which here is easily forded, and drew up on the other side, near some log cabins built for the accommodation of passing travellers. Here the horses were indulged in the luxury of stables, and Jim, after some foraging, returned triumphantly with a pumpkin pie for our supper. We chose a charming spot amongst the trees for pitching our tent, close to the water and far enough away from the civilized settlement.

Having only ridden about sixteen miles that day we felt quite fresh, and so putting on wading boots, and getting out fishing rods and tackle, we sallied forth in quest of the wily trout. It was very lovely. We waded down stream about a mile, and had a delightful swim in the swift, cold waters, while the sun began to set behind the great black pine stems and bathed us in streaks of golden glory. But not a fish did we even see.

As we were rather dejectedly wending our way homewards we caught sight of a dilapidated-looking old man with a white beard, and his battered felt hat stuck full of "flies," who was sitting on the bank watching us. A. went up to him and asked if he knew where we could get good fishing.

"Yes, I do; but I shan't tell you," he was answered very gruffly.

"We have come a long way, hoping for

some fishing, and have heard so much about the Snake," said A., in an insinuating tone.

Evidently something in his way of speaking seemed to strike the old man, for he looked up eagerly and asked, "Do you come from England?" and on hearing that such was the case he became most friendly, and invited us, then and there, to a "shake-down" in his tent, some eight miles up the river, and a day's fishing among splendid trout which nobody else knew about.

He told us he was an ex-doctor and had practised as a young man at Birmingham, but, as he suffered from his lungs, had been ordered out here, where he had been for fifteen years without a day's illness. "I should die if I went home, though," he added, pathetically. He seemed quite happy and contented, passing his summers in a tent with his dog as sole companion, and living almost entirely on the fish he caught; his winters being spent in one of the small towns of Idaho. He asked us all sorts of questions about the politics and general condition of the "Old Country," and seemed quite unaware of the changes that had taken place since he was there.

We arranged to go with him the day after the next, and to pitch our tent by the Snake as near to his camp as we—or rather the waggon—could get, and parted with much cordiality.

That night we made a grand bonfire, and as we were toasting ourselves over it (and listening to the howls of the cayotes), two guides from a passing stage, and a hunter, came up and began to chat with us. They seemed greatly interested in our movements, and gave us any amount of information about our route and what we ought to see. One of them was the best hunter in the place, and had just arrived with several elk and the skin of a fine cinnamon bear. He had been out with two gentlemen and a lady from California, and seemed to consider the lady the best shot of the party; at any rate two big elk had fallen to her share.

The next day, while A. and Beesley went off to replenish the larder with the toothsome prairie hen and wild-goose with which the place abounded, I went to make the acquaintance of the stage-innkeeper's wife, who, I was told, hailed from the "Old Country," and who lived in the log-cabin close by. She was washing the baby in a big outhouse, the walls of which were adorned with pelican skins and birds' wings outspread in artistic devices. So I sat down and helped in the operations, as she seemed rather "put about," having had to attend to a stage full of tourists who had just been breakfasting. She was a young and handsome woman, and was very anxious to know if I had ever been to Inverness, as she lived there as a child, and said she knew I was English by my looks. I told her, among other things, that I had a baby at home about the same age as hers.

"I guess you don't care for it much to leave it that awful long way," she cried, horror-stricken; nor did my virtuous explanation that I did not like being parted from my husband have any effect upon her.

"I guess I'd let *him* go!" she exclaimed, as she nodded her head to where her husband was cleaning his gun outside.

A. came back in the afternoon with a very good bag, chiefly wild duck, which made excellent stews—except that Jim was rather too lavish with the Worcester sauce.

We were well supplied altogether, as the hunter with whom we had talked the evening before presented us with a huge elk steak as we took our departure that afternoon.

We only made about eight miles this time, the road winding for the first half of the way through thick woods. These, however, diminished gradually into clumps of trees dotted about over grassy slopes, and we turned off the trail down one of them at a spot indicated by our ex-doctor, and soon found ourselves again on the banks of the Snake. Here we camped and enjoyed a quiet evening, mending our already torn clothes, and attending to various details of our domestic economy.

But *what* a business we had getting up

river to the fishing rendezvous next day! We foolishly took our horses (A. thinking I should be tired), and what between the rocky banks, which got more precipitous every minute, and the masses of fallen pine which completely blocked our way inland, we hardly made a mile in an hour, and had at last to wade Bolly and Snip through the river, keeping a sharp look-out for holes and boulders. Then, after we had met our old gentleman, who came part of the way to look for us, we had rather a nasty catastrophe as we were leading the horses up a rocky piece of bank to find a safe place in which to leave them.

A. was leading Snip along the top of the bank by the halter, and I was following with Bolly, picking our way among the trunks of fallen trees and loose rocks. Suddenly something frightened Snip, he plunged violently, and losing his footing rolled over, dragging A., who wouldn't let go the halter, after him. It was horrible seeing them disappear over the edge, and I believe I shrieked; A.

says something made a horrid noise. However, mercifully, they did not roll more than a few yards, as Snip struck against a pile of rocks and lay trembling all over, with his fore legs pawing the air. He was not much damaged ("they can roll a wonderful way down a precipice without scratching themselves," remarked our old gentleman, laconically), but A.'s right hand was in a dreadful state, the flesh literally torn from the bone by the halter, in his efforts to keep Snip back. Then appeared the advantage of having with us one who was a doctor as well as an angler, for, diving into an inner pocket, he produced some lint and bound up the wounds with hands that had by no means lost their cunning.

Well, we had very fine sport that day, the trout rising freely to a "yellow coachman," which seems a quite irresistible fly in these parts. Our old man made us promise to keep his happy hunting-ground a secret, though, while in those regions, as he complained very much of the way people ruthlessly destroyed the fish in other more frequented rivers, by dynamite and other foul means. "And they would soon empty our Snake if they could," he added, resentfully.

With two large bags of this excellent fish tied to our saddles we started on our way, the men having had orders to go some ten miles on and pitch our tent a little beyond the Lower Snake crossing. Unfortunately, we were obliged to wade the horses the whole way back to our late camping ground, owing to a tiresome deep hole in the bed of the Snake, which they absolutely refused to cross. This "doubling on our tracks" delayed us very much, and the sun had set as we turned at last into our proper course.

It was a perfect evening, of an intense, unbroken stillness; the air full of delicious aromatic scents, and the sky gleaming through the forest trees in streaks of a pale soft yellow. The scenery on each side of us had a curious effect, considering how wild was the region, an effect which we noticed several times. For it was as if we were passing through some great estate, and as if at every turn the house ought to come into view. Somehow, to our eyes, the stretches of smooth turf and the picturesque arrangement of the timber suggested a human handiwork; yet mile after mile we went and not a sign of human life did we see.

Now and then we caught a glimpse of the great gliding Snake, stealing noiselessly through the cedar and pine which fringe its edges in heavy masses and droop down low into its silvery waters. And once a dark object, a bear or an elk very probably, moved mysteriously through the underwood.

We reached camp at last in almost pitchy darkness, guided, however, by a huge fire which the men had lit to serve as a beacon from afar.

## CHAPTER II.

### A HURRICANE.

The whole of the next morning we were delayed by the horses, which, in spite of their hobbles, had managed to make off and could not be found. So, having enjoyed an excellent trout breakfast, we lay serenely on our backs in the shade, while the men scoured the country for the missing steeds. It is extraordinary how fast horses accustomed to being hobbled can get along. It really seemed to make very little difference to Billy, the roan waggon horse, who was always the leader in mischief, for, with his funny three-legged hop, he could go much faster than a man could run. Later on, we generally tied up Billy, as the other horses never thought of straying far from him. At last, after about five hours' search, the truants were discovered, and driven home, Jim astride the wicked Billy, waving his lariat right and left.

We soon saddled up, and started on our way, having about seventeen miles to make to our next camping ground. The forest stretched in front of us for the first hour or so, but it soon became thinner and the view more open beyond, till suddenly, turning sharply round the bend of a hill, we saw before us a great open valley, level and grassy, and completely walled in on three sides by ranges of mountains. To the east, however, it extended as far as the eye could reach on to a limitless prairie, out of which the white round peaks of the Three Tetons towered majestically all by themselves some seventy miles away. Through this valley, some ten miles long, lay our road, at the upper extremity of which we could see a glittering speck, Henry's Lake, a favourite resort of the hunter and angler. Flocks of wild-geese and countless heron were basking in this sunny valley, and a " bunch " of horses were browsing on the slopes beyond. It was capital " loping " ground, and we made very good time as far as Tyghee Pass, where the road leads out of the basin. Here was a stage resting-place, and we procured corn for the horses and milk for ourselves—the latter a rather rare luxury in the Park; and very unexpectedly a fat bundle of "mail" forwarded from Beavor Cañon by a passing team, the only communication we had with the outside world during our fortnight's ride.

As we ascended the steep slopes of Tyghee Pass, we kept turning back to admire the blue water of Henry's Lake, the abruptly rising banks of the Pass, covered with fir and maple, making an effective setting to the lovely, dreamy valley below; a contrast all the more striking as dark clouds were rapidly gathering in front of us and the wind was coming in fitful gusts down the Pass. It was extraordinary how quickly the storm gathered and how cold it became. As it was getting very dark we settled to camp at once, and chose the most sheltered spot we could find on the lee of a small hill.

But we had to content ourselves with a very cold and fragmentary supper that evening, as our fire was soon blown out and our food blown away! The tent was by no means fitted to withstand a gale, and though we pegged it down as best we could, the wind puffed it in upon us like a balloon, and we had to put logs of wood on our blankets to keep them down. Every minute the storm increased, till, as we watched by the dim light of our lamp, it seemed to shake our canvas walls as if in the hands of a fury, and the pole swayed to and fro as if it was drunk.

"It's going," I shouted, after a fearful gust, but A., who has a wonderful faculty for taking a nap under trying circumstances, did not reply. Just for a moment there was a lull, but only for a moment; then there came a great roar, and in a twinkling the tent was torn from the ground and hurled into the air, our blankets and various belongings whirling after it. Luckily, however, we had not undressed, so we were not in so bad a plight as we might have been. The men had taken refuge in the waggon (they generally slept rolled in rugs under a tree); but on hearing what had happened, they turned out and we took their places, having first secured a few of our wraps and our hay bags from the boisterous elements. Luckily, the canvas cover to the waggon buttoned well round, and protected us from the rain and hail, which presently beat down upon us like an avalanche. We managed to keep pretty warm and comfortable, as we were wedged in between a sack of flour and the tinned meats. The men, quite undisturbed by such a small catastrophe, crept under the fallen tent, which they had recovered, and seemed to enjoy excellent repose, though, when we peeped out at about five a.m., nothing could be seen of them but a little white mound, as the whole ground was covered with snow. Anything more wintry, one could hardly imagine. White peaks enclosing us on every side, trees bowed down with snowy wreaths, and a dark leaden sky overhead. No wonder we had begun to feel rather chilly, in spite of having pulled over ourselves a saddle and some provisions! We could not help laughing, however, at the injured and pitiable group of horses we beheld standing tails to storm, heads bowed down, Billy only unmoved and defiant, heading the group. Everything was soaking wet; the fire took a long time to light; and all our things had got more or less mixed up or blown away in the night. However, we maintained a cheerful equanimity, and before long were rewarded by seeing faint streaks of sunlight trying to pierce their way through the clouds; and by the time we were ready to start it was beaming forth gloriously, rapidly melting the snow and warming the chilly air.

# CHAPTER III.

### THE GREAT DIVIDE AND FIREHOLE BASIN.

We passed through several miles more forest that day—forests of black fir and spruce and of the tall white pine. On leaving them behind we entered upon vast grassy areas, from where could be seen far ahead the darkly-timbered mountains which flank the Madison Valley to the east.

The Madison is one of the chief tributaries of the Missouri, and has its source in the southern end of the Yellowstone Park, where it is called the Firehole River, rather appropriately, as it rises in the midst of geyser coves and boiling streams and springs.

As it enters the cañon by which it makes its way through the great Divide, it is joined by the waters of the Gibbon

River, the falls of which are one of the sights of the Park.

We had crossed the levels by about twelve o'clock and reached Manley's Cabin, as it is called. This is quite a large abode, with an open corral around it for the cattle, and is built of rough-hewn logs, the interstices being filled in with plaster. After many efforts, we at last attracted the attention of a very dignified-looking old lady in a black silk dress, who, we found afterwards, was the mother of the owner, lately settled there. She brought us out some milk, and asked if we were going through the Park, and if so, she said that we had better beware, as they had had a dead body brought back that morning.

"Dead body! of what?" we exclaimed, filled with awe.

"A man!" answered the old lady, solemnly, "killed by the dust! Nothing shall ever get *me* into that Park—not all the geysers put together," she continued impressively. And though we told her dust had no effect upon us, that we intended keeping off the trail, and that we were both very hardy persons, yet she paid no attention, but besought us to retrace our steps, evidently quite expecting to have our corpses brought back also.

We discovered later on that the "dead body" was that of a man far gone in consumption, who had insisted on going through; and the alkali dust, as might have been expected, caused inflammation of the lungs and killed him. For those who drive, this irritating dust, which accompanies your vehicle in white clouds, is a great drawback; but as we were riding we hardly suffered from it at all.

On leaving Manley's Cabin we crossed the Madison and were once more among the forests; forests of the dead more than of the living. Long intervals were sometimes completely covered with fallen and decaying timber: a strange and melancholy sight. All the pines die on reaching a certain height, and drop or are blown down, sometimes one by one, sometimes in whole tracts at a time. There they lie, piled up upon each other in various stages of decay; some with long lines of dust only, to mark out their forms, while pushing young sproutlings are filling up their places and flaunting green shoots over the poor mouldering remains.

Bolly, who would stand unmoved by the side of a geyser, thundering forth its two hundred feet of seething waters, had a distinct aversion to dead trees, and would shy most unexpectedly at some poor harmless looking fallen veteran, or gnarled old trunk that we passed.

We stopped to lunch on the banks of the Madison, a group of antelopes watching us from the slopes on the other side. Two sweet mountain parrots shared our meal, pretty grey birds with black tails and beaks, about the size of a starling. They were so tame, they actually pecked the bread out of our hands, and would sometimes try to seize a piece of meat out of the frying pan. We generally had a pair of them whenever we stopped to eat, and they and the blackbirds—which latter used to wait in flocks to clear up after us—and an occasional blue jay, were the only small birds we saw.

Some half-way across the valley we came to the military camp, which is established at the western entrance to the Park. Here we were accosted by two soldiers in uniform, who asked us if we had any guns to declare, as, if we had, they must be sealed up, to prevent our using them while passing through. For one of the most stringent Park laws is against molesting the game, or any animal within its limits; and though people are allowed to fish, they are supposed not to take more than is required for their party. If they are caught trespassing, they are promptly walked out from the nearest entrance, accompanied by a military escort, nor, under any pretext, will they be allowed to enter again. A very excellent law, and owing to its strict observance, the Yellowstone Park may be considered the animals' paradise. For here the almost exterminated buffalo can find a haven of safety, and the antelope and the elk, the big horned sheep and the mountain goat, can roam unmolested by bloodthirsty man. Even the bear too is not to be trifled with, and it seems quite a moot point if one is allowed to defend oneself from his embraces. We heard of a man who was caught in the act of shooting a grizzly within the limits, and who pleaded in defence that the grizzly had been stalking him, not he the grizzly, and as it had broken the rules by so doing, he was obliged to shoot it, as he could not walk it out of the Park in any other way.

As a rule, however, the bear does not seem to hanker after human flesh, and, unless attacked, when it defends itself with unequalled ferocity and courage, appears to lead a very harmless life, feeding on wild fruits in the summer, and on game and any carrion it can find in the winter.

We were close now upon the great Divide, as this Rocky Mountain barrier is called, up which the road ascends in steep zig-zags. There had been a forest fire extending for some miles on each side; a most weird sight. What once were trees were now bare charred poles, thrusting up straight and sharp into the air; or leaning against each other, poor shattered things, in helpless confusion; or tumbling together in blackened masses on the scorched-up ground,—a battlefield of slain. It was a heavy pull to the top, and in mercy to the willing but sweating Bolly and Snip, we walked up and insisted that Beesley, who was taking a nap in the waggon, should do the same. This was accomplished with some difficulty, as the man had been in a bad temper all day (owing to A. having remonstrated with him upon eating up our one and only pot of jam, a luxury reserved for me), and with sundry oaths declared he was not going to be " come over by any English boss," fingering his six-shooter in his trousers pocket the while. However, he thought better of it as A. remained quite firm, and at last sulkily dismounted.

We had a grand panorama from the top. The Madison winding through the valley like a thin silver line. Vast forests, some dark masses of green; others, charred black wastes, or peeled and white like armies of ghosts. Broad flat levels, misty distant valleys, range behind range of blue and violet hills; and not a sign, not a vestige of human life visible.

As we descended the other side, the forest received us again and closed in upon us; a forest so dark and impenetrable, few rays of sunlight could ever find their way within. We were about four hours riding through this, and it was evening when we at last emerged upon the Fire Hole Basin. Here stands quite a little settlement, consisting of the "Hotel," the stage agent's house, and a few primitive abodes belonging to men employed there during the summer months.

We were too tired to do anything but eat a hearty supper, though the peculiar sulphurous smell in the air, showing how near we were to "Wonderland" at last, made us long for morning to come.

We started forth, full of anticipation, to explore early next day. The Lower Geyser Basin, as it is called, extends some thirty or forty miles, it is covered with coarse grass, and is almost destitute of trees, although surrounded by them on every side. The geysers lie scattered about in groups, their presence plainly discernible by the cloudy wreaths of vapour which show up against the dark hills behind.

As we approached the geyser cones, the ground became quite bare and was covered with innumerable cracks and crevices, while the cones themselves and a few yards around them, appeared to be composed of pure white lime.

The first geyser we saw was the "Fountain," and though it only goes up about fifty feet—quite insignificant, compared with those in the Upper Basin—yet, it was our first, and thrilled us accordingly.

We tethered the horses to some stunted shrubs growing near, and stood eagerly watching while the "Fountain" began to boil up in preparation for action. The opening is in the centre of a pool about fifty feet in diameter, and projects from a sort of mound of rounded cushion-like formation, in which is the great orifice.

An angry spirit seemed at work, the water was dashing violently upwards, and the whole pool covered with foam. Then suddenly it would cease, then would begin again more furiously than ever. At last it became quite full of madly tossing waters, and then finally with a great roar up they shot in a beautiful column of some forty or fifty feet.

It played for several minutes, then lowered its crest and faltered, then shot up again, and so on for about half an hour. At length it stopped; with plaintive groans and gurgles the water sank out of sight, and the basin was left quite empty, so that we could distinctly see the curious white sponge-like formation with which it was lined. This formation, varying in colour and design, is a lovely feature of the geyser cones. No two are alike. Sometimes the glittering sides are of a delicate fan-like form; sometimes like clustering leaves, or escalop shells, even and regular as the diapering between gothic arches. The waters when still are of the purest and most exquisite colouring, a cobalt fading into purple, a vivid green melting gradually into yellow, and a thousand other indescribable hues.

Not far from the "Fountain" are some springs, the ground about which is of a blood-red colour, caused by some low form of vegetable growth.

On the other side are the "Thud" Springs, from which accumulations of steam burst forth every few minutes, with a mysterious muffled "thud," which seems to palpitate from some great living heart beneath. One of these is a dark green colour with fungoid-like formation around its base. Another is like the face of an old woman with a cap on, the scalloped edge of the basin representing the frills, the fissure the mouth, and two steam vents the eyes.

But the most curious of all were the Mammoth Paint Pots, which lie on the top of a white mound just behind the Fountain Geyser. The largest of these, called the Mud Caldron, is about forty by sixty feet, and is a boiling pool of pure white mud. A rather sickly-smelling steam is emitted from this, and the surface is covered with bubbles, which break with a funny *blob-blob*. All around are small holes full of what looks like whipped cream, of delicate pink and yellow shades, each blob-blobbing, and sending up little squirts of mud, most fascinating to watch.

We rode about half a mile beyond these to the Boiling Lake, from which clouds of steam were being wafted hither and thither in the wind. A quantity of little streamlets, over which our horses stepped very gingerly, rush down the sloping banks, carrying the overflow to the river; and poor, melancholy-looking dead trees, killed by the hot water, stood peeled and white and flinging out despairing arms around.

There were several minor geysers here, " Black Warrior," and " Young Hopeful," etc., but we had not time to see them all. One might stay for months exploring these curious sights without exhausting them.

In the afternoon we went to see the " Queen's Laundry," another pool of boiling water, which overflows into a series of smaller basins, divided from each other by lovely coral-like ridges of white formation. The water is very soft, and gradually cools as it flows from one pool to another, so that one can take a bath, or wash anything if so disposed. We had brought one of A.'s flannel coats, which had acquired a good deal of grime by the way, and this we washed very successfully by dabbling it about in pools of various temperatures. A. was induced, under great pressure, to put it on and sit in the sun to dry when we got home, and this excellent method quite prevented it shrinking.

Alas, that evening on saddling up we found Bolly's back was wrung; we had feared this would be the case, as the saddle did not fit him, though we had been very careful to pad it with horse-cloths underneath. For long rides like this, unless one can be sure of one's saddle, it is better to ride astride. Only it is well to secure a small, light saddle, as the big Mexican ones are too wide for a woman. It is not unusual out West for women to ride this way, and it certainly makes it far easier for the horse. I tried it towards the end of our journey, thinking the change would be beneficial to my steed's back. As the good little beast "loped" pleasantly along most of the way, I found it very comfortable; but I cannot answer for what would have happened if he had bucked or shied.

The weight of these Mexican saddles is terrible. A.'s weighed thirty-eight pounds, and was considered nothing out of the common.

It is curious to note how many of the customs out West are derived from the Spanish. Among these is the use of this heavy stock saddle, with its high horn and cantle, and the severe curb bit, on which all horses are ridden, whether they require it or not. We see it also in the stiff leather *chaperajos* of the rider, and the *cincha*, or saddle girth. Our guide was very fond of the word "cinch," and would use it very expressively to denote how he had the upper hand of a man.

"I guess I've got the cinch on him," he would remark, with a very knowing air.

Our horses were very much disfigured with brands. Bolly had indeed only three, and Snip, having lately come from the east, had only one. But the roan's flanks were quite covered, he having evidently changed hands pretty frequently; several of these marks too were reversed, which is a sign of new ownership. One sees all sorts of curious combinations in letters and figures, and as every brand is registered anyone imitating them is severely punished —if caught!

I was very sorry to change poor Bolly, but he certainly could not go any further, so the stage agent, with some difficulty, found another animal for us, a rather rough-looking beast, called Blaine, after the Minister of the Interior. This A. rode, I taking Snip, as he was the lighter of the two. We also made a change in guides, and were provided with an excellent pioneer, named Smithson, and his son Elijah, a lad of eighteen, to cook and drive the waggon.

Beesley was taken on to look after the spare cattle of Fire Hole. I think he rather repented his evil conduct towards us, for he shuffled up to our camp fire that evening, and after a long silence and much spitting into the glowing embers, said he guessed he wasn't much good at bossing the Park, and he wasn't going that line any more. This we felt was meant for an apology, so we wished him good luck, and parted quite amicably.

There was a sharp frost that night, and the ice was quite thick in our pails, but as we were over 7000 feet above the sea this was not surprising, and we were quite snug and warm in our tent, which we had had mended and patched up since the calamity of the night before.

We took an early swim in the Fire Hole River next morning; rather a curious experience, as it was quite warm, and very sulphurous. We were surveyed in speechless horror by some of the natives, who evidently considered us quite demented; and, indeed, Smithson afterwards affirmed he would rather face a grizzly than take a bath—at least a bath of that description. I do not think either he or Elijah ever took off their clothes the whole time they were with us. Certainly their toilet necessaries were extremely limited, and consisted of a mattress, two rugs, and half a comb, the latter kept jealously in Elijah's pocket, and lent to his father as occasion might require. Smithson, indeed, was much struck by all our luxuries. He did not at all approve of my sponge, saying it was a "ter'ble" thing to wash one's face in the Park. However, I did not find my complexion any the worse; though, of course, one has to be careful and use plenty of vaseline or cold cream, as the chemical ingredients in the water, and the alkali dust combined, are apt to cause irritation to the skin.

We started for the Great Geyser Basin about ten o'clock, forded the river, and following the road which led through the Fire Hole Valley, for about five miles, came to the Egeria Spring, better known, however, as "Hell's Half Acre." For here lies "Excelsior," the largest and most powerful geyser in the world, the thunder of whose eruptions can be heard for miles around; which sends up its boiling contents to a height of 300 feet, hurling huge rocks to all sides, as if they were pebbles, and flooding the river with such volumes of water that the bridges are sometimes swept away.

# CHAPTER IV.

### GEYSER-LAND.

But alas, "Excelsior" did not play for us. This monster geyser seems to take long intervals of repose, sometimes not erupting for several years. It had been very active the summer before (1888), and so was now resting from its labours. Smithson remarked to us for consolation, that it was such a "ter'ble" thing when that did "guise" we should all "wish we was in kingdom come."

We had met a very pleasant man, a settler in Montana, in the train from Salt Lake, and he had given us a great account of "Excelsior." He was hunting in these regions, long before they had been made a reservation, and when very little was known about them, except through vague rumours. He and his sons had been attacked by Indians and had taken refuge here, knowing what a horror all "dark skins" had of the place. They were congratulating themselves on having escaped, when from the huge pit near where they were standing came the most awful and deafening roar, as if the whole earth were going to blow up beneath their feet; and they, not waiting to see more, but thinking the world was coming to an end, turned and fled for their lives, preferring the tender mercies of the Indians to this new and unknown terror.

We tied our horses to some trees, and crossed the white chalky formation to where "Excelsior" lies, some 200 yards from the trail. Even in repose the giant geyser looked very awe-inspiring. It was belching forth volumes of steam, and as the wind wafted this to one side, we could look down into its great open mouth, some 250 feet in diameter, and about 30 feet deep. The water at the bottom was furiously boiling, and the edges of the huge caldron were jagged, and in many places undermined. Large masses keep continually falling in, and each year it gets larger and larger. Towards the river end the sides slope downwards, taking the shape of the hill over which the waters, streaming, and spreading, form terraces of a lovely rose and orange tint.

But if "Excelsior" is somewhat horrible, a few yards off lies a sight so entrancingly beautiful one feels that Hell's Half Acre contains an element of Heaven. This is a large pool called the Grand Prismatic Spring. Its surface is quite calm and unruffled, and its colours are indescribably lovely.

In the centre it is a wonderful dark deep blue, changing nearer the edge to a vivid green. Around the rim it fades into yellow—into orange—a ring of red—then purplish grey, the colours being intensified by the white coral-like deposit with which the pool is lined. One's eyes revel in these glorious hues, as they melt one into another, the whole glistening in its pure white setting like a liquid jewel.

But even lovelier was the Turquoise Pool, which lies close beside its Prismatic sister. It is about 100 feet square, and is of a blue so exquisite, so deep, so pure, the very sky—brilliant and unclouded, and thought so blue before—looked dark and colourless now. We stood fascinated. In its limpid transparency we could see every detail of the pearly shell-like formation beneath. No alabaster could be whiter, no sculpture more delicate than the curious wreathing devices, and foliations, which clustered round the rim. The overflow had worn a little channel, as it trickled down the slope, and enamelled it with pink, and orange, and yellow. It was fairy-like and it was weird. For a background were forests looking dark and cold against the white chalky plateau on which we were standing; while here and there around us stood poor white ghosts of dead pine, stretching out bare despairing arms,—punished for their temerity in daring to take root near the great Excelsior.

We had only about six miles to ride

before reaching the Upper Geyser Basin, and the road wound pleasantly over wooded knolls, and pretty sweeps of valley, misty columns of vapour rising up, like water wraiths from various boiling pools and baby geysers on every side.

At last we emerged upon this Great Geyser Basin. It extends about four square miles, and is completely hemmed in with forest-covered mountains. Through its centre runs the river, and on various little mounds and risings on either side lie the principal geysers.

On the lower levels are a few patches of coarse grass, and stunted trees, but everywhere else is the white limestone deposit, which forms a sort of crust round the cones. The place is full of surprises. Gurgling gasping sounds are heard under one's feet, and a rumbling in the air above. Hot stifling vapours assail one from out of innocent-looking little streams. One sits down on a cold looking rocky seat, and finds as one springs up again that it is scorching hot. One sees steam puffing out of little apertures no bigger than ant holes, and on picking up a piece of moss or a stone, one perhaps sets free a tiny geyser underneath.

Some of the geysers play every few minutes; some with several hours' interval; others with intervals of days or weeks. The most regular of all is "Old Faithful;" he never disappoints you, but sends up his graceful column of 160 feet, punctually every sixty minutes, thereby well meriting his name.

The "Grotto" was "guising"—the popular mode of expressing an eruption—as we entered the valley, and we hurried up to get a good view. The water was shooting upwards in two jets, from its grotto-like cone which stands about eight feet high, with a curious pillar on one side; and two little infant geysers were vigorously spurting away a few feet from it. The ground all around is covered with beaded silica which breaks up in slabs if disturbed. We looked down into the Grotto's curious arched cavities after it had ceased playing, lined with a smooth pearly formation, and into the black depths of its great funnel-shaped orifices, and wondered as to the extent of the terrible power beneath, to which it acts as a safety valve. The amount of time required for the construction of these curious tubes through which the waters are vented is supposed to be enormous; with the larger geysers ten or eleven centuries. A leaf or a twig placed where the spray of the water falls upon it is covered in twenty-four hours with a coating of silica, about as thick as a thin sheet of paper. At this rate it would take a thousand years to build up to the height of some of the geyser tubes.

Professor Tyndall has described in his lectures on heat considered as a mode of motion, the development of the Great Geyser of Iceland, which applies equally to all other springs of that kind. He says:—"It consists of a tube seventy-four feet deep and ten feet in diameter. The tube is surmounted by a basin fifty-two feet across. The interior of the tube and basin is coated with a beautiful smooth silicious plaster, so hard as to resist the blows of a hammer; and the first question is, How was this wonderful tube constructed—how was this perfect plaster laid on? Chemical analysis shows that the water holds silica in solution, and the conjecture might therefore arise that the water had deposited the silica against the sides of the tube and basin. But this is not the case: the water deposits no sediment; no matter how long it may be kept. It may be bottled up and preserved for years as clear as crystal, without showing the slightest tendency to form a precipitate. But if we place a quantity of geyser water in an evaporating basin the following takes place: In the centre of the basin the liquid deposits nothing, but at the sides where it is drawn up by capillary attraction, and thus subjected to speedy evaporation, we find silica deposited. Round the edge a ring of silica is laid on, and not until the evaporation has continued a considerable time do we find the slightest turbidity in the middle of the water. Imagine the case of a simple thermal silicious spring, whose waters trickle down a gentle enclosure; the water thus exposed evaporates speedily, and silica is deposited. This deposit gradually elevates the side over which the water passes, until finally the water has to take another course. The same takes place here, the ground is elevated as before, and the spring has to move forward. Thus it is compelled to travel round and round, discharging its silica and deepening the shaft in which it dwells, until finally, in the course of ages, the simple spring has produced this wonderful apparatus which has so long puzzled and astonished both the traveller and the philosopher."

Professor Tyndall considers the eruption of the geysers is owing to the entrance of steam from the ducts near the bottom of the tube, which elevates the geyser column to where the heat which it possesses is in excess of that necessary to make it boil. This excess of heat generates more steam and raises the column higher, the water below is relieved of pressure and its boiling point lowered.

More and more steam is generated, lifting the column higher and higher, until the whole upper portion of the water bursts into ebullition, and, mixed with clouds of steam, is projected into the air.

In Icelandic speech the word "geyser" means simply "rager," and is used to describe all turbulent fountains and pools. The most violent and noisy "rager" on the island being the great spouting spring near Haukadal, it gained for itself the title of The Geyser, and being the earliest known and most remarkable fountain of the kind, its native name was adopted in other languages as the generic name for all springs of that kind.

All around the Fire Hole Basin and the Yellowstone Lake are numerous extinct geysers. Some have been internally deranged by earthquakes, with others the waters have forced a passage elsewhere to other scenes of action, and some have died a natural death from decrepitude and old age. This latter takes place when the tube has reached such an altitude that the water in the depths below, owing to the increased pressure, cannot attain its boiling point.

At the upper end of the geyser basin stands a most civilized-looking hotel in Queen Anne style, and quite a sprinkling of people were to be seen about. Some of the female portion thereof were rather elaborately attired for such a remote portion of the globe; and one of them, clad in an elegant velvet dolman, high-heeled shoes, and much curled fringe, regarded my buck-skin leggings through her pince-nez, with cold and withering glances. Indeed, my appearance I generally found quite attracted people's attention from the geysers. I suppose if I had worn a blue plush habit with a locket and ribbon bow—as I saw a western damsel disporting herself in one day— I should have attracted no notice at all.

We pitched our tent in a clump of trees, near a tiny non-sulphurous stream, and a patch of grazing ground for the horses. Not far distant, the other side of the valley, were the soldiers' quarters; a detachment being kept here to guard the geysers and formations from the vandalisms of the public. Those individuals, therefore, whose souls delight in inscribing their names on, or otherwise defacing, the interesting works of nature about them, have to check these proclivities, or else they will very likely find themselves provided with a military escort and a summary ejection from the Park. The collection of specimens is not allowed either, though this is a good deal evaded with small pieces that are easily hidden. It was amusing sometimes to see a party of tourists, as a soldier appeared round a corner, instinctively put their hands behind their backs, or guiltily move in an opposite direction. That afternoon I unwittingly came within the iron grasp of the law. We had sallied forth after lunch for a geyser exploration, and I was looking into the pretty little cone of one of the "Cubs" which stand on each side of their big parent, the "Lioness" (so named because of the growling noise they make). This dear little "Cub" was boiling away at a great pace inside its pretty raised marble rim, and having heard what capital wash-tubs geysers made, I dropped in my handkerchief, and was quite absorbed in watching it being sucked down and then thrown up again, then sucked town to reappear once more. Suddenly a hand was laid on my shoulder, and a stern voice remarked, " Do you know you are breaking the rules ? " A., who had been quite lost in contemplating the " Lioness," now hurried up, and we both explained we had no idea washing handkerchiefs was included in the rules, and we repented deeply and would never offend again, etc. The man was evidently mollified and assured us that he was only doing his duty, and that that very morning a party had been marched out for throwing some eggs into " Old Faithful " to be boiled. However, he consented not to report us, and even condescended to try and rescue the erring handkerchief with my stick, which the " Cub," in a fright no doubt, had swallowed down and refused to eject. We poked about for some while and at last had to relinquish it, time being precious. We had not gone very far, however, when we heard someone running after us, and lo and behold! there was our good "Jonathan" quite out of breath, and holding up the handkerchief—washed snowy white—which he said the "Cub" had just disgorged.

We heard rather an amusing story of an Englishman (it would have been an American in England, I suppose) new to geyserland, who had had rather an unpleasant experience of one of the "Cubs." He had sat down upon the cone of one of them to wait for the "Lioness" to play, and as she did not seem inclined to hurry, he took a nap. Suddenly the "Cub" went off, after a few premonitory growlings, which he did not hear, and sent him flying from his seat, very much scalded and nearly frightened out of his wits.

We feasted on geysers all that afternoon. The "Castle," a pile of about twenty feet, looking something like a ruined fortress, which stands on a mound of grey and white deposit, went off splendidly. This is supposed once to have been the most powerful geyser in the Upper Basin, but though it sends up a vast mass of water and clouds of steam, it does not go higher than about fifty feet.

A little beyond the "Castle" is the "Morning Glory," a pool of a lovely pale blue, quite round and deepening in the centre, and with lovely white petal-like edges. Then there was the "Oblong' that threw itself up in a great splashing mass every four or five hours from a beautiful deep green pool. And the "Saw Mill," which sent up a pretty little jet every few minutes with a noise like a saw-mill working in a desperate hurry. The "Fan," too, is very pretty during eruption, spreading out in graceful fan-shaped fountains, and the sun shining through the falling spray gives an effect of showers of pearls.

Though we waited and longed, neither the "Splendid" nor the "Grand," which go up over two hundred feet, would perform for us. The "Giantess," which sends up the largest mass of water after "Excelsior," plays very seldom now. It is said to double the quantity of water in the river with its overflow, and goes up two hundred and fifty feet in one terrific ebullition.

But the geyser we set our hearts on seeing was the "Beehive," just opposite our camp, the other side of the basin. The cone, which really has all the appearance of a bee-hive in the distance, is about three feet in height and is beautifully coated with beaded silica. Its action is different to any other geyser, as the water is projected with such force from its comparaitvely small vent-hole, that it goes up in one perfectly straight pillar to over two hundred feet; and, instead of falling in floods on each side like the others, seems to evaporate into wreaths of steam and vapour.

Now there is a sure and almost certain method for inducing a geyser to play out of its accustomed hours, and this is done by what is called "soaping" them! It may sound incredible, but it is a well-known fact (which we attested on several occasions) that a bar or two of common yellow soap, cut up into pieces and slipped into a geyser cone, will have the desired effect in a very short interval. This is supposed to be partly caused by the soap creating a film on the water, which prevents the steam escaping. Smithson was as keen as we were that the "Beehive" should play. He assured us he had seen it soaped over and over again, with the most brilliant results.

So that night we sallied forth after all the world had gone to bed, armed with two large bars of Brown Windsor tied up in a pocket-handkerchief. The moon was shining fitfully behind the clouds, and now and then gleamed forth upon us, as, having crossed the river, we climbed up the white sloping sides of the "Beehive."

It was not due to play for several days, and as we peered down its dark funnel-like orifice, we could hear a soft peaceful gurgling, but nothing more; and even this quite ceased after we had slipped in the soap. We sat down then and watched. Presently it began to boil up—little by little—with a buzzing sort of noise as if it were hard at work. Every now and then it threw up a few squirts of water, and Smithson, who was getting very excited, laid his "bottom dollar" it was going to play. But, alas, though it seemed to be trying with all its might, yet it never quite got off, and having watched for nearly an hour, we decided to send Smithson back to camp for some more soap. Perhaps we had not put in enough, we thought, though Smithson assured us two bars was all it had ever wanted before. Well, in went the second lot, but with just the same result. It showed all the premonitory symptoms, boiled over, made a few gasps, and sent up a few small jets, and then gave it up. We got quite desperate at last. It was nearly twelve o'clock, and very cold, as a sharp frost had set in. We thought, however, we would have one more try. We hurried back to camp. There we found Elijah, stretched fast asleep before the smouldering embers of the fire. We cruelly awoke him, and made him produce the last piece of yellow bar, which we had hitherto thought necessary to leave for washing purposes. And to augment this, **A.** insisted on my bringing forth our few and treasured cakes of Pears. But no, even this last sacrifice was of no avail—that "Beehive" would not play! Smithson was furious, the first time it had ever refused for him; someone must have soaped it the day before, and if only we would wait it was sure to begin soon. But we decided we could not freeze there all night, even to see the "Beehive" display; and so dejectedly we made our way once more back to camp. Just as we were going off to sleep we heard a roar—something was "guising" at last, but we were too tired to stir even if it had been "Excelsior." The next morning, however, just as we were dressed, we heard the roar again, like the sound of a sudden hurricane or of numberless distant guns. "She's off —the 'Beehive's' guisin'," shouted Smithson, and off we dashed, helter-skelter, arriving breathless, but in capital time to see a grand eruption.

It was terrific. It seemed as if the whole hill-side must be blown out by the tremendous force with which it burst forth. Higher and higher it soared, in one great round perpendicular column of over two hundred feet, clouding the whole sky with masses of spray and steam. Presently a gust of wind blew up and carried the topmost wreaths in feathery masses over the valley, and we were able to stand quite close to lee of it without getting a drop upon us. It played for about twenty minutes, then wavered, trembled, and finally subsided with sundry gurgles and groans. As we came away, several people who had hurried out from their beds to see the sight, began making remarks on the curious fact of the "Bee-hive" playing before its proper time. "That's been soaped," said a man who belonged to the place, looking suspiciously round, at which we appeared innocently surprised.

Before leaving, while I took a rest in the waggon, A. and Smithson went off to see the "Black Sand Basin" and the

"Devil's Punch Bowl." A. came back very enthusiastic about these lovely pools which lie about half a mile off the trail. The former is a beautiful blue spring, surrounded by high banks of black sand, and the latter a rainbow-coloured pool of boiling water, surrounded with an incrustation of different shades of red and orange. We had not time to visit the "Lone Star Geyser" (though much attracted by its *name*), as you have to ride about six miles over fallen timber. The cone is quite unique, we were told, being ten feet high and beaded with sparkling geyserite.

We had to retrace our steps to the Fire Holè Basin to regain the trail for Yellowstone Lake, therefore we decided to camp at the former place that night, as our next resting place was to be on the banks of the Yellowstone River, nearly thirty miles distant.

There were several lovely spots we should have liked to visit; Kepler's Cascades, about two miles east of the Upper Basin, where the water dashes through a deep, rugged, and very narrow cañon; and Shoshone Lake, lying in a hollow between heavily timbered hills; but we had to limit ourselves somewhere.

## CHAPTER V.

### BIG GAME.

We made an early start next day, and had a good bit of hard climbing, as we had to cross the high " Divide " or range of hills, through which, further on, the Yellowstone Cañon is cut. On each side of us lay dead and prostrate pine, crammed in masses among the living, forming a very labyrinth of desolation. Through a gap amongst them, now and then, we caught a glimpse of the lovely bluish-purple Rockies, the higher peaks white with snow. Near the summit we passed a dear little lonely piece of water, called Mary's Lake, its edges strewed with fallen pine. We also passed Sulphur Lake, from which a very nasty odour arose, and further on Alum Creek, which our horses, though very thirsty, sniffed disdainfully and would not taste.

The other side of the Divide was undulating table-land, and here again were those curious park-like effects, and for miles we passed in and out of grassy slopes, surrounded by impenetrable woods, not once seeing a living creature larger than a chipmunk, though Smithson said the place was full of bear, and we came across buffalo and elk trails continually.

We were very anxious to see some big game, " roaming in their native forests free," and so Smithson proposed we should make a détour some miles off the trail, as we should then be more likely to see some. But not for all the " big game " in the world would I go that détour again.

First of all we stuck in a swamp, A.'s horse going in up to his girths, and Smithson's roan pitching him head over heels in its struggles into the black mud and rank grass which surrounded us. As for me, seeing their fate, I slid off Snip just in time as his fore-legs sunk suddenly, up to his nose, in the treacherous ground. We floundered about for some minutes, and at last succeeded in dragging the frightened beasts on to terra-firma; and the next mile or two, by skirting close to the trees, we managed to keep clear of pitfalls. But swamps were mild compared to the terrors of the tracts of white chalky formation we had to cross. Boiling pools of sulphur all around us, steam belching up from the hoof-marks of our horses, as each step broke through the thin crust, while horrible groans and rumblings filled the air. It was all very well in the geyser basins, where the ground was hard and well tried by other feet. But here it was more than probable no human being had ever penetrated, or at any rate very few. Snip did not like it at all, and trembled with fright, as every step nearly sunk him over the fetlocks in the hot mud. I gathered a little comfort from the fact that A., who turns the scales at nearly twice my weight, was on in front, and therefore what bore him might be supposed to bear me. But all I know is that it did not, and that Snip and I had a horrid flounder in the steaming mud, near a wicked-looking gurgling hole, which the others passed quite safely. After that, being hot and thirsty we (Snip and I) nearly killed ourselves by drinking out of a lovely little purling stream, only Smithson rushed up just in time and said it was full of arsenic.

We were rather disreputable-looking objects, when we emerged on to the trail. We had seen no big game, and we were covered with swamp mud, and further ornamented with white chalk. Then, when we caught up the waggon, Elijah informed us he had passed five splendid elk, close to the road, the largest he ever saw!

But our longings to behold big game were fulfilled that night, though not quite as we expected.

We pitched our tent on the Yellowstone banks, by a lovely bend that carried it through great rocks further down. Behind us were thick forests, and in front long blue lines of hills. It looked a splendid place for trout, with its deep pools and gravelly shallows, so, though it was getting dark, A. brought out his rods, and in a very few minutes had secured some fine big fellows, which were delicious, grilled for supper.

The men had stupidly left the axe behind at our lunching place, and so it happened our tent was not very well pegged down that night. However, as it was clear still weather, we thought it did not matter, not dreaming of other alarms. I was rather tired and slept soundly, and it must have been about one o'clock when I was awakened by funny little squeaks near the tent, and I heard the men from the wagon, about ten yards off, calling out and trying to frighten something away. This ceased for a little. Then presently I heard something creeping round the tent, and some more squeals. The lamp was dimly burning, and I turned it on the entrance, which was the unpegged part. Something was squeezing itself under the canvas, something about the size of a badger, black and smooth, and with a sharp little nose. I turned the lamp full upon it, and we stared at each other, both much surprised.

My stick was close at hand, so I whacked on the ground, upon which the little beast turned tail in a hurry, and scuttled out as fast as it could. A. by this time was awake, and professed to be much surprised that I, who was so fond of live creatures, should object to the poor little thing. "As if it would have hurt us," he remarked, as he turned over and went to sleep again. However, dearly as I love the animal world, I prefer not to have unknown species thereof rambling about my sleeping apartment, and so I lay awake on the chance of having another visit. Before long I heard something walking about with heavy lumbering gait, some few yards off. Then it came nearer, walked slowly round the tent, sniffing along the bottom, and brushing up against the canvas as it passed. With some difficulty I awoke A.

"There's a wild beast outside!" I cried, "and it's trying to get in—what shall we do!" A. replied that he would rather be eaten than wake up, and that it was most likely a poor little mink or inoffensive creature of that kind, and I had better go to sleep again. But at that moment it began to move once more, there was a shuffling at the entrance—a great big something bulging it out as it tried to poke its way through. Then, as we watched, horrified (having no guns in the tent), we saw a large brown head thrust through the insecurely fastened opening. "It's a wolf!" I shrieked, "and it wants to eat us!" And we seized our sticks and made a terrific noise to frighten the monster. He certainly was surprised, for he quickly withdrew his nose, and we heard him sloping off. I was dying with curiosity to see what he was like, and at last summoned up courage to peep out. It was early morning, and a faint cold light made everything distinctly visible. There, squatting a few yards off, was our visitor, watching us, and trying to make up his mind whether to investigate further. I had no desire for a closer acquaintance with him, however, and beat on the sides of the tent with my stick, and yelled at him in a way that evidently struck terror into his savage breast, for he turned tail and trotted off, and I lost sight of him below the hill. After this we barricaded the entrance and made it as secure as we could, and A. promised to keep watch for the rest of the night. However, I had not the smallest inclination to close an eye even, and as soon as it was light enough we got up and roused the men to prepare breakfast. We found they had had a lively night also, as they had had mink after the fish, and our big brown visitor also, which latter had been attracted by the elk steak. They declared it was a wolverine (a cross between a wolf and a fox), which is a very cowardly sort of brute, and rarely shows fight or attacks mankind. But they confided in A. afterwards that it was really a cinnamon bear, but that they did not like to tell me for fear I should be too much alarmed to sleep in the tent again, whereas nobody minded wolverines. However, as I told them, one was quite as alarming to me as the other, though, now it was all over, I was not ill-pleased at having seen one of these interesting beasts so near; for many people go through the Yellowstone without seeing a vestige of a bear, especially if they keep on the trail.

The cayotes and wolves are much scarcer than they were, as the cattle-men have poisoned and killed them in large numbers, owing to their depredations among the young calves, etc. The mountain lion also, a horribly savage beast, something like a small panther, has been trapped and hunted down to a large extent, and is not often seen. The lynx, we were told, is the only beast that would attack one unprovoked, and it has been known to stalk a man for miles and spring upon him from behind, or from the branch of a tree overhead.

There are several species of bear in the Rockies. Amongst these the Grizzly, or Hog-back, is the largest and most ferocious. His strength is so enormous, and his tenacity of life so great, that, though his body may be riddled with bullets, he will, with undaunted determination and courage, hurl himself upon you again and again.  The only instantaneously vulnerable spot is in the forehead, and it requires a cool head and a steady hand to make sure of hitting it.  For, if you miss, you are done for, unless well supported, or with a haven of refuge at hand.  And if this refuge is a tree, some discrimination is necessary in the choice thereof, for if large enough he will soon be after you; and if too small, he will station himself at the bottom and endeavour to gnaw through the stem, or with his iron-muscled paws will wrench it from the ground.  Therefore, if you are fleeing from a bear, choose a medium-sized tree, too large for him to tear down, and yet not large enough for him to climb, for if his arms overlap much he cannot get his grip—and you are safe !

The Silver-tip is rather smaller than the Grizzly, and has longish brown hair tipped with silver, and a silver frill round his throat.  Then there is the Cinnamon, the Black, and the Smut-face.  None of these seem to interfere with you if let alone, and if you are careful in the cubbing time not to take up or fondle any dear little cubs you may see about. That summer a man was watering his horse in a small gully, and seeing two of these little brown balls waddling up the bank by themselves, took one in his arms. It gave a little cry, and in an instant there was the spring of a dark body from behind some bushes not far off, and a huge paw had struck him lifeless to the ground.

But I must not wander off on bear stories. That day we had grand sport—if hauling in fish as fast as you throw the line can be called sport! And indeed, after catching about thirty splendid trout, weighing from one and a half to two pounds apiece, in less than an hour, we felt it was becoming butchery. It was extraordinary how fast they bit. We had waded to the middle of the river near some tiny rapids, shallow and gravelly, and we could see them swarming up stream by dozens. They did not heed us a bit, and rushed after the flies, two or three to each. A. sometimes landed two at a time, and I, who had never fly-fished before, had only to hold out my rod to catch one. Any child could have done as well. They all appeared fine fish, though some we found were wormy. It is rather a curious thing that the trout above the Falls, and in the Yellowstone Lake, should suffer from these nasty little parasites, while those below the Falls are not affected at all. We found that the wormy ones were not nearly so game as the others, but would let themselves be reeled in with very little resistance; their flesh also was inclined to be flabby. These worms generally appear under the pectoral fin, and will sometimes nearly eat it off.

But I must not forget to mention the Mud Geysers. These lay about a quarter of a mile from our camping ground. We went to see them directly we arrived, and again the first thing in the morning, watching them with a sort of fascinated loathing, till the sickening steam drove us away. The chief one we heard had not been seen playing for some while, but we soaped him, and he played for us, both now and afterwards on our way back from the Lake; and, so quickly did he gratify us, we half forgave him his sinister and horrible appearance. This geyser lies in a hollow, bare and caked with clay, and looked very much like a pool of mud. From its surface, as yet quite still, arose clouds of dense grey steam. We slipped in two bars of soap, cut up quite small, and sat down on the bank to watch. In a few moments it began to bubble and to boil. It was as if some invisible hand was kneading it up, or some horrible unclean spirit was furiously at work beneath the dark slimy mass. Waves of mud clashed together in angry squirts; these grew higher and higher, more and more furious, till at length up went a great seething volume of thirty or forty feet. Ugh! It made us shudder, so ghastly, so black and hideous was the effect. As it subsided there were noises from beneath like vomitings from some giant throat, with beats and throbs as from a monster heart; then it sank down, smoothed itself, and once again was calm and still.

But the Belching Spring, higher up on the hill side, was even more thrilling. Imagine a great hole, thirty feet deep, volumes of steam curling up its steep sides. At the bottom of its huge yawning mouth waves of evil-looking mud are for ever belched forth with a horrible gulping noise. It sucks them back, then belches them forth again, relentlessly, never ceasing, hurling its slimy masses against the walls of the pit, and splashing high up almost to the brim. We lay full length along the edge peering over for nearly an hour, with something of the sensation a bird must feel when under the cobra's eye. We expended several bars of soap upon the "Belcher," but he sucked them down into his horrid mouth and was quite unaffected thereby.

# CHAPTER VI.

### YELLOWSTONE LAKE.

WE saddled up that afternoon and had a glorious ride of about sixteen miles to the Yellowstone Lake.

The trail ran pretty near to the river, which grew gradually wider and wider, broadening out here and there and leaving little islands in the midst. Endless masses of dark forest were on our right, and endless hazy stretches of distant Rockies far over the valley on the other side. Everywhere wild and free, untrodden and untouched!

We made a détour through the woods, thick with fallen pine. As long as there was foot room between the trunks, the horses would walk quite unconcernedly over them, picking their way very cleverly, and making funny little hops over the very big ones.

As we turned on to the trail again we came suddenly upon a poor dead horse, just dragged to one side with its legs sticking on to the road, the fresh blood still oozing from its distended nostrils.

"Over driv'—broke its heart," remarked Smithson, laconically, and when we exclaimed at its being left like that, he seemed quite surprised, and "guessed folks hadn't time to be buryin' horses," they had just to "git through" as quick as they could. We afterwards passed several more left in the same way, in various stages of decomposition, some half-eaten by wild beasts, a sickening sight.

One of the most painful things out West is the way the horses are treated. The cayouse is looked upon as naturally bad-tempered, and to be broken by fear only. It spoke volumes to see the way both Blaine and Snip threw up their heads in terror if we tried to stroke their noses, or lifted our hands suddenly near them. We very soon gentled them, however, and, in time, they would let us do anything with them. As no grooming apparatus had been provided in our outfit, we sacrificed our one and only clothes brush, and while the men looked on in wonder at our "sweatin' ourselves for nothin'," as they expressed it, we brought quite a shine into Snip and Blaine's rough coats.

Horses cost very little out here. Bred in large quantities by the Indians, they are sold at prices varying from fifteen to fifty dollars. You can buy a good average beast for thirty dollars, and will generally find that your saddle costs more than your horse! Many people think it better value, in riding or driving tours, to buy their horses and sell them again afterwards. It certainly costs less, barring accidents.

We reached the Yellowstone Lake in the evening, and camped in a little knoll by its side. This is the largest lake in North America of so high an elevation, being nearly eight hundred feet above the sea. The water is of a silvery grey colour, clear as crystal, and of enormous depth. It had a peculiar spirit-like aspect. The mountains which surrounded it to the east looked like grey phantoms in the evening light. To the west, great forests cast black shadows, contrasting sharply with the pure snowy peaks behind, while densely-wooded islands looked like spots of ink upon its pearly surface. We longed to visit some of these islands, as we heard their shores gleamed with brilliant pebbles, crystals, and bits of obsidian. Some of these concretions take the most curious forms, such as cups, boxes, spoons, etc. There are also numerous small geysers, hot pools, and paint pots. One geyser pours its boiling contents into the lake, others spring up from underneath its bed and make rings of bubbles on its smooth surface.

Alas! next day a mist hung over all, enwrapping the fairy-like scene in impenetrable gloom. So we had to give up the rowing expedition we had planned (if we had been able to secure the one and only boat on the lake), and determined to push on to the Yellowstone Falls, and give ourselves a little longer time there.

We followed the same road back for about eleven miles, passing our late camping ground by the river, where we stopped to lunch and revisit the Mud Geyser.

On turning into the road that leads to the cañon, we left the trees behind, and passed over undulating ground covered only with the sweet scented but monotonous sage-brush. Now and then we crossed a little creek bridged by round pine-logs, placed side by side on trestles without any attempt at making them secure, the consequence being they generally rolled about in a manner not altogether pleasant, and one of the horses' legs was pretty sure to go through as we passed over them.

Before entering Hayden Valley we crossed Sulphur Mountain. This is a great cone-shaped pile of pure sulphur, the colour of gamboge, and encrusted with the loveliest yellow crystals. It was very hot,—as we found when we sat down on a crystal ridge to watch a big sulphur pool, which lay in a little dip in the hill, boiling and spluttering forth its yellow streams. At every little crevice steam of a sulphurous odour was puffing forth, and we amused ourselves by making little vent-holes with our sticks to help it to escape.

We soaped that sulphur pool, too, with our very last bars, in the hope it might turn into a geyser. But though at last in desperation we cast in a pound of butter, some cart-grease, and a piece of cheese, not even these dainties had any effect upon it, though it sucked them greedily into its funnel-like throat. All it would do was to send up a little squirt from its centre. It seems always to be in a furiously boiling condition, its overflow streaming in numerous little crystallized yellow channels down the hill-side, over which our horses very gingerly picked their way.

# CHAPTER VII.

### THE GREAT CAÑON AND FALLS.

A few miles beyond the Sulphur Mountain, we came once more to the Yellowstone River, which here was broad and clear, with peaceful grassy banks. Its bright green waters, though quite unruffled, were flowing very swiftly, however; and then gradually, as the valley begins to contract lower down, they gather themselves together to burst their way through the great jagged rocks which form the entrance to the Cañon.

The road follows the left bank of the river for many miles. Slowly and surely, though almost imperceptibly, we seemed to be sinking deeper into the earth, and the pine-covered banks seemed to be rising higher and higher on either side. But we turned off and were enveloped in trees before we reached the Upper Falls, and had a last glimpse of the river, narrowed and white and foaming, pent in by towering cliffs, rushing madly on its way.

The trail wound gradually uphill through the forest and then to an open clearing, where was a corral for horses, and further on a series of huts and tents which formed the "hotel."

It was dark by the time we had fixed on our camping-ground above the Upper Falls, the majestic roar of which sounded solemnly in our ears. We waited for the moon to rise, and then set forth to feast our eyes on the great Cañon and the Lower Falls, the highest falls of that volume of water in the world.

We followed a path cut out of the mountain side which leads almost to the top of the Cañon, a pretty steep ascent. Thick trees on either side obscured the view, until presently, following the guide, we crawled along a narrow ridge that stood at right angles from the trail, at the end of which was a pinnacle of rock, where one could cling and look up and down and all around.

THE FALL OF THE YELLOWSTONE.

We were speechless—thrilled!

Beneath us yawned 2000 feet, black, immeasurable. The moon glinted on innumerable overhanging fragments and columns of rock, some sharp and pointed, like cathedral spires, piercing up from the depths below. Dark pine forests fringed the edges, and here and there, hurled against the rocks in their fearful descent, lay fallen trunks—headlong—stretching forth gaunt arms of horror. Twenty-four miles that awful chasm splits its way through the heart of the mountains. A mighty river is frantically bursting through its far-away depths, so far, no sound of its rushing can ever reach the ear.

And then the Falls! Imagine a vast white gliding mass, a wall of snow, pouring itself between two great shoulders of rock in one splendid plunge into the black abyss, a plunge of nearly 400 feet, amidst wreathing and wafting clouds of spray and wind-flecked foam. It was a sight before which Niagara, Shoshone, all we had ever seen, or dreamed, of sublime and wonderful power and beauty, faded and was lost. Awe-stricken and breathless, how insignificant we felt clinging there!

By daylight it appeared even yet more wonderful, because of the entrancing colours of its marvellous setting. For on every side are crags of the most weird and curious forms, sometimes bathed with crimson as with blood; sometimes splashed with shades of orange, or ribbed with yellow and brown. There are rocky ledges smoothly laid with vivid green as with a painter's brush. There are chalky beds of mountain torrents now dry, or glacier-worn channels, trailing in sparkling whiteness to the distant river far below. Across and athwart it all lie black shadows from rugged battlements and towers, riven and torn by a giant power and poised upon the sharp descent. And the eagles hover and circle over the pinnacles and spires, on the points of some of which they have built their nests. And above the falls gleam the rapids, as, lashing themselves against the walls of rock on either side, they madly tear along. And a rainbow ever comes and goes, and irradiates with its bright colours the great white, solemn, plunging mass, and melts into the misty wreaths of foam. And—one feels one will never look upon such a scene again. It is Nature's masterpiece!

Dr. Hayden, in his report on the geology of the Park, concludes that the Cañon is one of erosion, and has been cut by the waters of the Yellowstone. The rocks are igneous, and are stained by the oxidization of minerals and by hot springs. There is a high ridge on the east fork of the Yellowstone, called Amethyst Mountain, in the exposed strata of which are imbedded the petrified remains of ancient forests. Some of the huge trunks are forty and fifty feet long, and in some places they stand upright on the ledges, "like columns of a ruined temple." The branches, roots, and fruit are also found in the strata, and in some instances perfectly preserved leaves have been discovered.

The Washburn Range extends to the north-east of the Grand Cañon, the two highest peaks of which are Mount Washburn, 10,346 feet above the sea, and Dunraven's Peak. We had intended crossing the former of these, as we heard the grandeur of the view from its summit is unrivalled; but there was a rumour that the trail was blocked with fallen trees, so we gave it up.

The next day we forded the river with some difficulty, about a mile above the Upper Falls, and explored the other side, a thing very few people had ever done, Smithson remarked, which was satisfactory to hear. We tied up the horses and walked for a long way by the broken Cañon side. Its vastness seemed to grow upon one, as we caught glimpses of the river between the jutting crags, diminished so as to appear like a thin blue ribbon fluttering in the breeze. We loosened huge boulders and rolled them over, and watched them crashing down, bounding from rock to rock, till they looked no larger than pebbles and were lost to view. Not the faintest sound of their reaching the bottom could one even hear.

So much time was spent over this fascinating occupation it was quite late when we reached camp. Here we were greeted by Elijah with the pleasing information that the waggon horses had been stolen and not a trace of them was to be found. It was no good doing anything that night, but early the following morning the men, having fortunately secured two mounts from the "hotel," started in pursuit, and guided by the discovery of the tracks made by Billy's off hind foot, which had lost a shoe, they found them at last in a little gully, into which they had been driven, about eight miles distant, and brought them triumphantly home. Smithson shook his head darkly as to who were the thieves; he evidently had suspicions, though he would not commit himself.

It is seldom any robbery, except that of horses, takes place within the Reservation. The Yellowstone tourists do not, as a rule, burden themselves with valuables, and of this the "highwaymen" are well acquainted.

The summer before we were there, however, the Yellowstone mail was robbed in a very daring manner. It happened to be carrying the tempting sum of ten thousand dollars to a man in the Teton Basin, in payment for a herd of cattle. The money was put in a treasure box, which was rather a risky proceeding, one would think; but it is often sent this way out West, where banks are few and far between. The robbery was carefully arranged. Two men hid themselves about sixty miles from the station, and a third remained to watch the transfer of the treasure from the railway agent to the stage company. Having witnessed this, the man rode night and day, and reached the hiding-place well in advance of the stage. The three of them then burst forth upon it as it came up, and, covering the driver with their six-shooters, demanded the treasure. This was instantly produced, for, as usual in such cases, no one was prepared. Having broken open the box and secured the bags of money, they procceded to relieve the trembling passengers of their valuables, and then, in the words of the narrator, ordered the driver to "git," and he "got."

They had a start of four days while a posse of men with the under sheriff was collected for their capture. They were followed through the mountains for a week, and were caught at last, after a tremendous struggle, in which one of them was shot dead. The treasure, which had been buried, was eventually recovered, not without some difficulty, however, as nothing would induce the men to confess where it was hidden. At last two of them were put together in a cell, and someone was stationed to listen to them night and day. By the end of a fortnight a clue to the hiding-place had leaked out, and the treasure was found and restored to its owner.

This seems the only exciting incident of the kind that has been perpetrated within the Reservation; though there are plenty of thrilling tales to be heard of the regions all around.

# CHAPTER VIII.

### A DIGRESSION ON "HOLDING UP."

A FEW years ago the cowboys were a good deal rougher and wilder than they are even now, and to "hold up" a team or railway-cars was common sport. It is still a not at all unusual thing out West for a train to be "held up." The marauders, choosing a dark night and a lonely spot, show a red light for danger, whereupon the train is slowed off, and they can mount with ease, enter a car, and, levelling their "six-shooters," order all hands to be "held up." As they are, as a rule, dead shots, this is generally acceded to with the greatest alacrity, and while one covers the conductor, the others go round and empty the pockets of the passengers.

The day before we left for Salt Lake, the "Rio Grande" was held up by two men only; so chivalrous were they, however, that not a thing was taken from a woman, only their own sex were disturbed, though they shot the engine-driver who showed fight, and rifled the mails and luggage. Unfortunately, we had no interesting experience of this kind to relate, though we made every preparation when travelling in those regions; I taking all the valuables, leaving A. a few dollars only to hand to them, as we thought it might arouse their suspicions if he were found quite moneyless.

An Englishman living in Colorado told us he had been full of boasts he would show a little more spirit than to let himself be "held up" so easily. But when put to the test one day, as he was walking along a lonely mountain pass, he found his hands were elevated pretty quickly upon being covered with the muzzle of a revolver, suddenly produced by a man who was riding past, and who ordered him to "hold up," while he relieved him of his watch and money. On these occasions, too, in order to prevent your getting at your revolver—if you have one—you are generally ordered to walk on for some distance with your hands up, while the desperado stands covering you till you are out of sight; and this, our Colorado friend told us, was the most creepy sensation he ever experienced.

This same acquaintance warned us that we had better look after ourselves at Leadville, a little mining town in Colorado, 12,000 feet above the sea, to which we were journeying, and that if anyone asked us the time after dark, it would be as well to pull out our revolvers instead of our watches. It is of Leadville, by the way, the well-known story is told of a man performing on the piano at a party, with a label pinned on his back inscribed with: " Gentlemen are requested not to fire at the performer, he is doing his level best."

Montana has long had a bad name for the ferocity of its cowboys. Very often, after receiving their pay, they would gallop into a little town, crowd into the beer saloon, place the glasses and bottles in a row on the counter, and taking potshots at them, very often end up by shooting through all the windows and lamps, and a person or two besides. In fact, a cowboy who had not shot his man was thought very poorly of. Still, it must be said in their favour that, though they would be only too ready to pick a quarrel over any trifle and shoot you, yet they would be very friendly and hospitable until ruffled. The Vigilance Society, however, a band of the better class of law-abiding inhabitants, has done great good by following up and securing the murderers and bringing them to justice, and so now the state of things is much more civilized.

We heard some very amusing stories about the doings of the "boys," as they are called, from a Mr. Reed, a very agreeable man we met later on, who acted as sheriff in some of these lawless regions for some while—adventures more amusing, doubtless, to listen to than to experience!

He told us he was sitting one day in a little barber's shop, being shaved, in a small town near Pueblo. Suddenly a rather ferocious-looking man clattered in, all leather and spurs, and with his belt full of six-shooters.

"Now, then," he cried, "you just vacate that chair, or I'll blow your brains out."

"You're welcome to it in a few minutes, when I'm through," replied Mr. Reed, in as calm a tone as the circumstances permitted of.

"What, you suppose I'm going to wait, do you!" roared the man, pulling out his revolver. Mr. Reed began to feel decidedly uncomfortable. Dignity forbade his vacating his chair, and yet if he didn't do so the chances were he would be shot as he sat. As for the barber, so great was his fright, he had dropped the razor, and was making frantic signs in the glass for Mr. Reed to get up.

However, just at this trying moment the latter was seized with an inspiration.

"I rather think you don't know where I come from," he remarked, quietly.

"What's that to do with me?" replied the man, gruffly.

"Well, I think you'll consider it has. I come from Christian, Texas."

The man's face was suddenly transformed. He strode up to him and gave him a tremendous slap on the back, and nearly wrung his hand off.

"Come and have a drink and a talk," said he. "I'm at the hotel."

"Well," said Mr. Reed, "I've business for a couple of hours, then I'll come."

His train left in half an hour, however; "and never having been to Christian, Texas, in my life, I took care not to miss it," he remarked, in conclusion.

This Christian, Texas, is renowned for its wickedness and shootings. Its inhabitants are the wildest set out West, and are mostly dead shots. A person from this interesting locality, therefore, was always treated with great respect by other " boys," and was certain not to be molested by them, unless under very provocative circumstances.

The cleverest " holding up " we heard

of was performed on the Denver Bank. Everyone was full of it when we were there. It was done in broad daylight, by one man only. He walked into the bank during the dinner-hour one day, and asked to see the President in his private room. He was shown in, and, as the door closed, he quickly locked it with one hand, and with the other covered the President with his revolver, and threatened to blow his brains out, unless he wrote him a cheque for fifty thousand dollars. The President, completely unnerved, assented. He was then made to go and present the cheque to the cashier for the money, which was delivered to the man, who then walked calmly out—backwards—his eye on the President—and was never heard of again.

Smithson was very fond of relating thrilling tales to us over camp fire, a good many of which, of course, we took with a grain of salt. He seemed to think about as much of a " holding up " as we should of an orchard robbing; but then a life or two lost does not count for much out West.

His aversion to the Mormon persuasion was intense, and his face of disgust when he discovered he was eating Mormon food was very funny. He informed us his father was a Mormon, and had had eight wives. Upon the prettiest and youngest of these " old Brigham " had, however, cast covetous eyes, and, stating that it had been revealed to him that she was to be Abraham's wife in the next world, appropriated her to himself for this. His own mother died when he was a child, and, according to his account, he does not seem to have fared very luxuriously at the hands of the other seven. " Bacon rinds is what I was raised on," he would remark sardonically, "and what they did to them Christians, folks talks of, is nothin' to the ter'ble things them Mormons did to me when I left them and married a Gentile wife. I jest had to *git*, and come out here to Montana."

Among other things, he told us he had been offered a Post Office by his " party," when they were in office, but as he could only read or write with difficulty, he had conscientiously refused. These important qualifications seem sometimes regarded as quite a secondary consideration to whether a person may be a Democrat or a Republican, which system, as we discovered, does not conduce always to the due delivery of one's letters.

This is quite a trifle, however. Such details as one's life, or even one's letters, are not considered of great importance Far West!

# CHAPTER IX.

### NORRIS BASIN.

About twelve o'clock that day we started for Norris Basin, fifteen miles distant. We followed the edge of the Cañon for some way, up and down, between rocks and trees, such awful dizzy heights, I fain dismounted and led the callous Snip, heedless of A. who remarked that I was much safer on his legs than my own. Then we turned off and took a short cut over some wild stretches of valley and forest.

As we were "loping" the horses across one of the grassy slopes, Smithson, who was in front, cried out suddenly, "Four bears, as I'm alive—if that ain't derned luck!" And sure enough, there, about a hundred yards in front of us, were four big brown lumpy-looking things, watering at a little stream that flowed at the foot of the tree-covered hills. We were so excited, we cast prudence to the winds and galloped straight for them, leaping the brooks that crossed our path, and coming right upon them as they were ponderously making their way back to the woods. The horses were rather frightened, though not as much as one would have expected, and we succeeded with some difficulty in keeping them up to our "big game." The four great beasts turned round and eyed us solemnly for a few moments, then snuffing the air disdainfully, as if we were beneath contempt, slowly shuffled off. We followed them a little way, until they disappeared among the trees, but they did not hurry their pace. It certainly was a very thrilling sight, and we heard afterwards that to see so many full-grown bears together was most unusual. They were Silver-tips, three males and a female, and were of a dark-brown colour with silvery ruffles round their necks. The female was of a lighter shade than the others, and rather smaller. She kept well in the rear, and when they turned to go, led the way, followed by the three males close abreast. I suppose if we had in any way molested them, our lives, even on horseback, would hardly have been worth a moment's purchase; but we only wanted to look, and so we were safe!

We turned on to the trail about eight miles from Norris Basin, a broad, graded, road, which made us feel within reach of civilized regions once more, and consequently rather damped our spirits. It led gently down hill through an endless forest of bastard fir, or bull pine as they are called, their slender upright stems packed so thickly together only a small beast could have squeezed itself amongst them. We entered another beautiful cañon as we approached Norris Basin, with huge perpendicular cliffs and the Gibbon River dashing turbulently close to the roadside. The cascades here are very lovely. The water sweeps down a gentle incline of about eighty feet of moss-covered rock, spreading itself out like a sheet of frosted silver. Leaving this behind, we soon entered, descending still, upon the Norris Basin, and from the curling wreaths of vapour arising from white barren patches amongst the trees, we could see we were in Geyserland once more.

We camped near a winding stream, cool and clear, across the Norris fork of the Gibbon River, and were much disturbed all night by the horses belonging to some other camping party, who seemed to mistake our tent for that of their owners, and came trampling and whinnying round, evidently wanting to be fed. Smithson, who spent most of his night trying to induce them to roam elsewhere, "guessed t'other folks were short of corn, and had driv' 'em over river to us"—which seemed to us very reprehensible conduct.

There is a neat little stage house at Norris Basin, where we procured some fresh milk, a great luxury; and having had an icy cold bath in the stream (making S. and E. "chatter all over to see us,") we sallied forth to explore the Norris Geyser. The road led through the barren formation where they chiefly lie, some extinct, some just bursting into life, others dying away. The "Constant" was sending up energetic spouts, and the "Minute Man" showered a lovely fountain regularly as its name denotes. From a black-looking hole on the side of a mound a volume of steam bursts forth every few seconds with such a blast, it is as the roar of countless engines letting off steam together. Then there was a furiously boiling mud-pot, sending up tongues of liquid, pale drab mud, writhing and twisting as if it were some tortured spirit. Hot and cool pools lay close together. The Emerald Pool was like a fairy's grotto, lined with lovely coral-like forms, and tinted with the most exquisite emerald hues.

We were very anxious to see the "Monarch" display, as it is the largest in these regions, and owing to the shape of its orifice it goes up in a long thin sheet unlike any other. It lies in a hollow scooped out of the hillside, shaped like a sort of throne, and is supposed to play every twenty-four hours. We determined to see it, even if we waited all day, and seated ourselves to watch, sending Smithson back for our lunch. I believe after an hour or so of expectation we had a nap, not having enjoyed very excellent repose by night. We suddenly found ourselves very wide awake, however, for a stage full of tourists came clattering down the hill, singing at the top of their voices some very convivial air. They drew up and alighted near the "Monarch," but were soon herded off again by their driver, who intimated that they would lose their lunch if they did not hurry. (In many small American hotels, unless you keep hours you are in danger of starving, as the cook seems to ply other trades between meals, and locks up the larder and every edible substance, and takes away the key.) A good many tourists we met at the Upper Geyser Basin bemoaned to us that they had not seen a single big geyser perform, and as the stage that arrived at the Grand Cañon one evening, departed pretty early the next, they did not see very much of the falls either. No wonder they found the Park rather disappointing!

They had hardly gone five minutes when the "Monarch" began to bestir itself, and we retired to a safe distance. It boiled up, slopped over several times, and the most uncanny noise proceeded from its long thin mouth. Then it burst forth, up and up, widening and spreading, soaring higher and higher—like glistening icebergs endowed with life—like snowy mountains leaping into being. The sun was shining from behind and turned it as it fell into showers of glory, and the whole sky was obscured by the clouds of spray. It played for nearly an hour, pouring forth a river of water; then it lowered its crest and dwindled into intermittent and attenuated forms, like white ghosts trying to escape and ever falling down. Then, at last, with a sobbing noise it sank to rest and peace.

Though the "Monarch" is not so high

as the "Beehive," or even "Old Faithful," it is of much greater width and volume of water; indeed, we considered it quite the most beautiful geyser we had seen—the last and the best.

## CHAPTER X.

#### MAMMOTH HOT SPRINGS.

From Norris Basin to Mammoth Hot Springs is about twenty-one miles. Until lately the trail led over a very steep mountain 3000 feet high, but now the Government Engineers have constructed a new road through the Cañon of the Gardiner, making it quite an easy journey.

We made very good time the first seven miles after leaving the Basin, crossing by a gently sloping pass, the divide which separates the waters of the Gardiner River from the Gibbon. A lovely sheet of water spread before us as we left the pass, and extended for more than a mile along the side of the road. Beaver Lake it is called, as it was formed by dams constructed across the Green River by these clever little beasts. Among the grass-covered ridges, and along the swampy edges of the lake, wild geese and crane were splashing, while ducks and waterfowl innumerable were basking upon its serene surface.

Rising from the eastern shore of Beaver Lake are the Obsidian Cliffs, "unequalled in the world," as the guide books say. They certainly are very curious, these walls of black and violet glass, bright and glistening, and streaked here and there with red and yellow. To make a road through this barrier was a great difficulty. It was only accomplished by lighting fires upon the huge masses of glass which blocked the way, and then when these had sufficiently expanded with the heat, cold water was poured upon them, causing them to fracture into fragments. This obsidian is a species of lava, and is extremely difficult to cut. It was much valued by the Indians for arrow-heads and tools, specimens of which are still picked up.

Our road extended now for some miles through a valley or sort of plateau surrounded with hills, amongst which stood forth the Sepulchre Mountain, looking in the distance as if it were covered with huge grave-stones. We turned off to the right at the head of this valley, and entered upon a narrow pass which leads through the Cañon of the Gardiner, the pass of the Golden Gate, so called because the face of the rocks is flecked and spotted with the brightest and most vivid yellow. The road is blasted from the side of the Cañon, and seems to hang over the depths, where, far below, the Gardiner River is flowing. We looked back and back regretfully, as we descended the sharp zig-zags that led us from the receding walls of the gorge to the valley where lie the springs, and not far beyond the limits of the Park. It was the last day of our ride, and the golden gate of fourteen happy days was almost closed upon us. Even the men were regretful, and said they'd "never bossed the Park so friendly and comfortable before," which was refreshing to our melancholy spirits.

As we entered Mammoth Springs we perceived with some revulsion that we were indeed in the gay world once more. Smartly attired ladies were strolling about, and we passed a group of young men in tennis flannels, with rackets in their hands. It nearly took our breath away when we rode up to the hotel, and saw at what a palatial building we were to be " located." There was an imposing façade of about four hundred feet, with a broad terrace, where beauty and fashion were disporting themselves in all their glory. I descended from dear Snip's back under their astonished glances, and for one weak moment almost wished my attire was more feminine, and my buckskin leggings not tied up with pieces of string where the buttons had come off.

We had quite a business getting our kit together, as it had got rather mixed up with the hay which had burst out of our mattresses. However, we were clear at last, said good-bye to our faithful steeds, and watched them, and our outfit, wend their way to the camping ground where they were to pass the night before starting on their return journey.

We were supplied with a huge bedroom, fitted with electric light, and with such spacious wardrobes we quite wished we had some clothes to put in them. The hotel holds three hundred "guests," and it seemed pretty full. The people were very amusing to watch, they were such a funny mixture. Officers in uniform, from the depôt, looking very immaculate; business men taking their holiday in black coats and top hats; cowboys and stage-drivers dropping in for a dinner and a wash after "rounding up"; and every description of tourist and traveller, in every sort of "get up" imaginable. The women were most of them very smart, some with low dresses, and flowers in their hair. These, however, we heard, were not "transients" (the American term for the sojourner of a day or two), but were boarding there for the summer.

The manager was very civil, and took us into his private office for conversation, and blew up the manager of the Cañon

"Hotel" by telephone, on our complaining of his refusal to sell us some salt because we were "campers out" and brought him no profit.

Next morning, having paid into Smithson's hands the money for our outfit, which he was to take back to Beaver Cañon, and said good-bye to him and Elijah with violent hand-shakings and complimentary speeches all round, we started to explore the springs.

These lie in about four hundred acres of white travertine formation, much the same as in the geyser regions, but the springs themselves are quite different. At first sight they look like lovely marble terraces one above the other, rounded and escalloped. But on approaching them one discovers that they are formed by clusters of little basins full of hot water, each ornamented with a delicately moulded rim, and with curved and fluted sides. The water trickles over the edges from one to another, blending them together with the effect of a frozen waterfall. One can walk up between the terraces, where the

THE MAMMOTH SPRINGS.

water no longer flows and the formations are crumbling to decay, and admire the lovely colouring with which some of the basins are coated; cream and salmon, green and yellow. The Minerva terrace is one of the most perfect of these; it is fed by a powerful spring laden with oxides, with which it paints the walls of its basin in richly shaded colours of cream, pink and copper. But the most beautiful of all are those that are pure white; some of which are called the Pulpit terraces. No human architect ever designed such delicate flutings and such intricate mouldings as adorn these wonderful formations. But they glisten coldly in their spotless whiteness, for they are dead, and the waters that built them up have gone elsewhere, and left them to a gradual, though as yet far-distant, decay. There is hope for them still, however, they may live again; fresh springs may break out, and with their deposits build up what is crumbling away. If not, they will some day be like the many terraces higher up the hill, that have quite lost their lovely forms, and in the earth-filled basins of which dwarf pine and cedar have taken root, and grown, and flourished.

The chief spring is the "Cleopatra," which lies in a mound of deposit about forty feet high. Down its sides, where the water overflows, are numerous smaller basins, fringed with pure white stalactites. Some of the cones are very curious. There is one that points up like a sort of finger; it is forty-seven feet high, and it took fifty-four centuries to grow. They seem to increase at the rate of about a foot a century, so one can judge their age pretty accurately. We saw several infant cones only two or three centuries old; others that must have been growing for thousands of years.

There are all sorts of surprises—pits, grottoes, and caverns—as one explores further up amongst the ridges and hollows and white ghostly-looking rocks. There is the Stygian Cave, the mouth of which is covered with the corpses of insects and birds caught and killed by the poisonous vapour whilst flying over; and further on is the deadly River Styx, with expiring creatures fluttering on its banks. There is another cave with dark mysterious chambers, and the Boiling River flowing underneath; and beyond, a narrow fissure, where you hear its waters pouring through a bed of sulphur and arsenic with a hissing, grating noise. It would take weeks to exhaust the wonders of these Mammoth Springs.

We had heard a rumour that there was a hot lake where we could have a swim, and so had brought our bathing dresses with us. After much searching we found it at last, lying in a hollow surrounded on one side with bushes and stunted trees. We entered with some caution, not wishing to be boiled alive, but soon discovered where its spring lay and kept at a comfortable distance, where we could just bear ourselves, taking refuge along the more tepid edges when we got too hot. It was altogether great fun; though the air felt dreadfully cold when we came out, and we were quite glad to hurry home to lunch. As we were discussing this said meal, I began to extol the delights of our bath to our table companions, but my remarks were received rather coldly, and I noticed the horrified glances cast upon me by some ladies opposite. Having terribly shocked the modest Mormons by bathing in Salt Lake with bare arms and without stockings, I thought my attire had something to say to it,—perhaps I had been seen by one of them. But as I was looking through the local guide book I learnt the awful act I had committed, as after describing Bath Lake and expatiating upon its charms, it remarks with much pathos, " Ladies, alas, cannot even *see* it, owing to the male bathers that occupy it exclusively." By the time I had discovered this, however, our audience had vanished, so I could not retrieve my character by explaining that not a vestige of any sort of bather did we set eyes upon.

After lunch we walked down the valley to the Gardiner River, where it flows side by side with the Boiling River, the latter joining it further on. It is here that one can catch one's trout and cook him without changing one's position,—standing on the bank between the two streams and popping the fish caught in the Gardiner into the hot river the other side, where he is done to a turn in about five minutes! We should like to have tried this for ourselves, but the Gardiner had been overfished that season, and we had not a chance.

The next morning we started by stage for Cinnabar, about six miles distant, to which place the Northern Pacific runs its branch line from Livingstone. The road passes through the Gardiner Cañon and is flanked with magnificent cliffs and pinnacles of rock on either side. In the distance is Sentinel Peak, with its human-like face uplifted, staring into the heavens; and Mount Evarts, which is always capped with snow. Then through Gardiner City; the city consisting of a dozen or so wooden shanties and log-houses, chiefly burnt down, as they had had a fire the night before, and the belongings of the inhabitants were strewed about all over the road. We nearly ran over a billiard table, and just escaped a serious accident over some pots and pans.

The train was waiting for us at Cinnabar and took us through the Lower Cañon, where we had a grand view of the Rockies, with Emigrant Peak 13,000 feet high, the sombre gulches of which are rich in gold; and passing the Devil's Slides,— long crimson-stained courses, formed ages ago by streams of lava pouring down from the heights above. Glaciers have stranded gigantic boulders between the slopes, some of which, wind and water worn, take curious and fantastic forms like unto beasts and birds and living things.

We had to wait several hours at Livingstone to be taken up by the mail from San Francisco, and employed our time in searching for a buffalo robe among the hunter's stores, for which the place is renowned. We secured the only one we could find, for sixty dollars, a handsome hide, though only that of a cow (a bull's, we were told, would cost over a hundred dollars). A few years ago we could have picked up either for four or five dollars, but so successfully has the buffalo been shot down and slaughtered, that it is well nigh exterminated; it is said, indeed, that there are hardly 300 head left in the whole of the States.

It has been estimated that as many as four and a half million were killed between 1872 and 1874 alone. The skin hunters used to start out in parties with a regular outfit of waggon, tent, cook, etc. When they got near a herd they would encamp and prepare for the slaughter. One hunter was sufficient, the rest being skinners, as the only important point was to get to leeward of the herd and to keep well hidden from view; for this exceedingly stupid beast, as long as he smelt or saw nothing, would appear quite callous to noise, and would go on browsing contentedly with his brethren falling dead around him, displaying only a mild curiosity at their death struggles. Thus very often as many as fifty or sixty beasts would be shot down without a change of position. The bodies were usually left to the vultures and cayotes, only the skins being secured. Their bones, that used to whiten the prairie, have been now collected and sent off for manufacture into buttons and various other things. In Canada, as skin-hunting is prohibited, there are a few hundred head still left, but even these mysteriously dwindle, as do those within the Reservations in the States, and soon the buffalo— as well as the Indian—will have succumbed to the advance of the civilized (?) world; and cowboys and horses, cattle ranches and beer saloons, will occupy the vast ranges where both once used to roam.

As we were sauntering about after our purchase, we were invited, by the owner of another hunter's store close by, to come and see a mountain lion, the only one, he asserted, that had ever been tamed. It was in a little back room, chained to a strong iron staple in the floor, around which it was pacing, uttering low growls. It appeared very like a small panther, and seemed anything but "tame," snarling at us as if longing to spring. It was in awe of its master, however, and cowered down each time he cracked his whip. He made it do several tricks with a dear retriever dog, who did not seem half to like it. "Come and kiss Miss Pussy," said the man, and the dog went up to it and laying his paw across its neck licked its face. He then put a piece of meat on its nose, and told the dog to come and fetch it away. "He doesn't care for this part," remarked the man; "she's had him by the throat once or twice." However, this time Miss Pussy allowed her dinner to be abstracted with only a snarl of disapprobation. "I wouldn't take a thousand dollars for her," continued Miss Pussy's master, with great pride. "Barnum'd give his eyes to have her! Just look at her iron paws, one blow 'ud lie you dead as mutton—what, you brute—you would, would you!" (Miss Pussy tries to gnaw his boot but is lashed off.) "Yes, I take her out walking in the mountains sometimes, and with her chain off, when we are out of the town; only I take precious good care I follow her, not she me," he added, with a laugh.

In spite of these attractive traits, we were not sorry to say good-bye to Miss Pussy, as we heard the sound of our approaching train, and hurried off to secure a "state room" to ourselves, as we had a journey of two days and nights before reaching Chicago.

American travelling is, certainly, very comfortable and well arranged. Our state room, with a lavatory and hot water, was upholstered in terra-cotta plush, was lighted by electric light, and could be warmed, if necessary, by hot pipes. Our beds had spring mattresses, and we had an attendant ever ready to bring us iced water, books from the library, fruit, or anything we desired. Excellent meals were served in the dining-car (on some lines they give you a hot bath), and one could get plenty of exercise by walking through the cars, all of which were connected by little bridges. However, in spite of all these luxuries, we gazed sadly and regretfully on the fading-away peaks of the wonderland in which we had passed so exceedingly delightful a time, feeling that never, wherever we might go, should we behold so many marvels, or such grand and beautiful sights; never should we feel within us such an exhilaration of health and strength, such a capacity for enjoyment, as in this entrancing Yellowstone region.

## CHAPTER XI.

#### LOST IN THE YELLOWSTONE.

It is only of late years that travelling through the Yellowstone could be accomplished without great difficulty. It was, indeed, an undiscovered country about twenty years ago. There had always been vague stories and rumours current about it, but, owing to the cordon of rugged and lofty mountain ranges by which it is enclosed, it remained for a long time unknown. Every attempt to penetrate this region from the east and south-east was an utter failure, as the snowy glaciers of the Wind River Range formed an insurmountable barrier.

It had therefore to be entered from the west.

The first successful attempt was made in 1870, by some of the officials and leading citizens of Montana, led by General Washburn. During thirty days they explored the cañon of the Yellowstone; then, crossing the mountains to the headwaters of the Madison, they visited the geyser regions of Firehole River, and ascended that stream to its junction with the Madison.

One of the most remarkable experiences of long-sustained privation ever made known, was endured by Mr. Evarts, a member of this expedition, who was separated from the rest of his party for thirty-seven days. He has written a thrilling description of all the perils he encountered, perils enhanced by the extraordinary and phenomenal nature of his surroundings. It may be interesting, as a close to this account, to follow him in his wanderings; in a slightly abridged form, however, as he is inclined to apostrophize upon, and moralize over, his adventures, a little too frequently for the cold-blooded and critical reader's taste.

The unfortunate man somehow lost sight of his companions while they were endeavouring to make their way through an immense tract of fallen timber. Separations had, however, often occurred before, and he rode on in the supposed direction they had taken, quite confident of meeting them or of finding their camp.

Darkness soon overtook him in the midst of the dense forest, and, after selecting a suitable spot for spending the night, he picketed his horse, made a fire, and went to sleep.

The journey of the day before had been up a peninsula, jutting into the Yellowstone Lake, on the shore of which they had intended to rest. The next morning at early dawn he started in this direction, hoping to find his friends encamped on the beach. But the trees were so thick he made very little way, and the falling foliage had obliterated every trace of a trail. He was obliged to dismount every now and then to examine the ground, and while doing so, unfortunately, did not always take the precaution of holding or of fastening up his horse. Startled at something, on one of these occasions, it suddenly made off, and disappeared amongst the trees, and though he tried to follow it up, and spent the whole day searching for it, yet, he never saw a sign of it again. As his blankets, pistol, fishing gear, matches—everything except his clothes, two knives, and an opera-glass, were attached to the saddle, his feelings can well be imagined.

After wandering till dusk, he found himself back in the place from which he had started, and the uncomfortable conviction began to force itself upon him that he was lost—a hundred and fifty miles from the nearest abode, without food and without fire, or means, as far as he could see, of procuring either.

These disturbing reflections, combined with the barking of the cayotes, and the howls of the grey wolf, did not conduce to very pleasant repose, especially as he mentions being naturally timid in the night.

The next morning he decided to cross the peninsula centrally, hoping to strike the lake shore in advance of his companions near the point of departure for the Madison. He felt very faint and hungry as he scrambled through the timber-entangled forests, and looked eagerly about for any possible food. His attention was presently attracted by a small green plant of a very bright hue. He pulled it up by the root, which was long and tapering like a radish, and tasting it, found it palatable. It was a kind of thistle, and this not very nourishing vegetable formed his almost sole source of food for the thirty-seven days of his wanderings.

At last he emerged from the forest into an open space at the foot of the peninsula, where lay a beautiful lake of about twelve miles circumference, surrounded by a rim of smooth white sand. It glittered in the sunshine with what appeared to him an almost unearthly radiance after so long a journey in the dark forest.

The vapour from innumerable hot springs, and the jet of a geyser rose in wafts to the sky. Swans, otter, beaver, and mink, sported unfrightened around him. Elk and mountain sheep stared at him without a vestige of fear.

Rising as it were from the depths of

the water, stood the loftiest peak of a vast range of mountains. This he recognized as Mount Evarts, so named, a few days before, by General Washburn, in his honour.

But he was too jaded and anxious to really enjoy this novel and beautiful scene; as he remarks pathetically, his tastes were "subdued and chastened" by the perils which environed him, and he longed only for "food and friends."

A large stream flowed from this lake which he conjectured to be Snake River, and, thinking he had discovered the source of the great southern tributary of Columbia, he christened it Bessie Lake after his only daughter, which name it still bears. At first he was rather afraid of meeting Indians, but now he felt even a Bannock or a Crow would be welcome— anything in the shape of a human being. He had a great disappointment at Bessie Lake in this respect, for as he stood looking over the smooth grey water he thought he saw a canoe coming towards him rowed by a single oarsman. But, alas! as he rushed joyfully to meet it, he found it was an enormous pelican, which flapped its dragon wings in mockery and then slowly flew away. As night approached he made a little nest for himself under the fallen branches of a tree and went to sleep. He was soon aroused, however, by shrill screams, like a human being in distress. It was the screech of a mountain lion, so alarmingly near it thrilled him with horror. He yelled at it in return, seized the branches of a friendly tree, and swinging himself up, scrambled into a place of safety.

The savage beast was sniffing and growling below, and making the circuit of the tree as if to select the place to spring from (the Rocky Mountain lion is something between a wild cat and a panther, and is a good climber). Hoping to frighten it, he threw down pieces of branches at it, which only made it the more furious, and it howled and lashed the ground with its tail. Then he tried silence, and sat for a while perfectly still, the lion imitating his example, which he seems to have found even more trying to his nerves than its roaring, as it was quite dark, and he could not be certain where it was. At last, luckily, the evil beast gave him up, and springing into the thicket was heard no more. He was so weak and exhausted he says he almost tumbled out of the tree, and, incredible as it may seem, crept back into his old bed and was soon lost in slumber.

He was awakened in the early morning by a terrific storm of mingled snow and rain with a high easterly wind. He scooped a little hole in the ground and covered himself up with fallen boughs as best he could, and there he lay for two days, his only food consisting of a little benumbed bird which hopped within reach, which he seized, killed, and devoured raw.

On the morning of the third day, taking advantage of a lull in the storm, he rose and started in the direction of a large group of hot springs which were steaming under the shadow of Mount Evarts. He thinks he travelled about ten miles, but before he had gone half the distance the storm recommenced. Chilled through and through and with saturated garments, he at last reached the welcome springs, and flung himself down on the warm encrustation which surrounded them. He found a few thistle roots growing near with which to appease his hunger; and then, selecting a spot between two springs just far enough apart to afford heat to his head and legs at the same time, he built a little bower of pine branches, and spreading the ground with moss and leaves, stowed himself away till the end of the storm.

Close at hand was a small round hole, containing a boiling spring. This made him a convenient dinner-pot where he could cook his thistle roots, and, except for his frost-bitten heels, he seems to have been pretty comfortable.

The storm soon became more and more furious, and he describes pathetically his semi-parboiled condition owing to the condensations of steam from the springs. However, it was better than being frozen, and he says, in contrast, he quite liked the sensation.

It appears to have flashed upon him, while watching a gleam of sunshine play upon a pool of water, that his opera-glass lens might provide him with fire. It seems somewhat strange that this very obvious method did not strike him before. He describes his joy when, on holding the lens over a chip of dry wood, he saw the smoke begin to curl and sparks arise. Now he could command warmth and cooked food, and he felt immensely cheered. All thoughts of failure were abandoned, and, in spite of his weak and attenuated condition, he felt he was saved.

Misfortunes, however, came thick and fast. A sudden heave whilst asleep broke the crust on which he reposed, and the boiling mud beneath scalded his hip severely. This, added to his festering, frost-bitten feet, delayed him several days longer, though he busied himself the while with preparations for departure.

Having lost both his knives, he made a rather ingenious substitute by sharpening the tongue of a buckle. With this he cut off the upper parts of his worn-out boots and made a pair of slippers, fastening them on with strips of bark. Then, with the ravellings of a linen handkerchief and the same magic buckle-tongue, he mended his clothes. Finding a piece of red tape in a pocket, he manufactured a fish line, and a pin made him a very fair hook. By sewing up the bottoms of his boot legs he made a pair of pouches in which to carry his food.

Thus accoutred, on the morning of the eighth day after his arrival at the springs, he started in a course directly across that portion of the neck of the peninsula between him and the south-east arm of the Yellowstone Lake. It was a beautiful morning, the sun shone bright and warm, and he felt quite exhilarated as he plodded on his way. But, alas, there was a change in the wind before many hours had passed, and an overcast sky quite obscured the sun, so that no fire could be obtained. A freezing cold night set in, and a bleak hillside, sparsely covered with pine, afforded, as he remarks, poor accommodation to a half-clad, famishing man. He describes it as the longest and most terrible night of his life. It was only by the most active exertions that he could keep from freezing. On dawn approaching he retraced his steps to Bessie Lake, and building his first fire on the beach, remained by its side to recuperate for the next two days. He now gave up all hope of finding his friends, and made his plans quite independently of them. There were three courses open to him. One was to follow Snake River one hundred miles or more, to Eagle Rock Bridge; another to cross the country between the southern shore of Yellowstone Lake and the Madison Mountains, by scaling which he could reach the settlements in the Madison valley; and the other to retrace his steps along the line by which he had entered the country.

The route by the Madison, though obstructed by the mountain barrier, was the shortest, and so he was tempted to adopt it,—to his cost, as he afterwards found.

Filling his pockets with thistle roots, he started for the nearest point on Yellowstone Lake, travelling all day with pain and difficulty over fallen timber and through dense thickets and forest. This time he took the precaution of utilizing his lens early in the afternoon, keeping a flame alive by means of a succession of brands. As night approached he lit a fire, in the only clear space he could find, the gleams of which played luridly amongst the impenetrable gloom, a gloom rendered all the more terrible by the constant scream of the mountain lion, or howl of the cayote and wolf. The burn on his hip was so inflamed he could only sleep in a sitting posture, leaning with his back against a tree. To complete his woes, while snatching a fitful slumber, he fell forward into the red-hot ashes of his fire and badly burnt his hand.

A bright and glorious morning succeeding the dismal night, cheered him considerably, and he resumed his journey towards the lake in better spirits.

Another day of toil brought him about sunset upon a lofty headland jutting into the lake, and commanding a magnificent view over the mountains and valleys. In front of him, about fifty miles away, rose the " arrowy peaks of the three Tetons." On the right "rolled the picturesque range of the Madison, scarred with ravines, gorges, and cañons." All the vast country within this grand enclosure, with its lakes and forests and hot springs, lay spread out before him, and, in spite of his miseries and suffering, he felt lost in the splendid scene.

Carefully holding his lighted brand, he climbed down the stony headland to the beach, and lighted a fire. The sand was soft and smooth, so taking off his stiffened slippers, he wandered barefoot along the shore, collecting for the night. He gathered a big pile, and then sat down to eat his thistle-roots and rest. But, as usual, he was hardly allowed to enjoy an hour of peace before another misfortune overtook him. He had stuck his slippers into his belt for safety, but on wishing to put them on again, found that one was lost. It was getting dark, and the idea of passing the night in a freezing temperature with a bare foot was not pleasant to contemplate. Besides he knew he could not travel a day without it. He searched for ever so long in an agony of fear, poor man, feeling his life depended on that shoe. At last he found it, lying under a fallen branch, with what joy, as he says, no tongue could describe.

The next morning he awoke feeling quite refreshed, and, after eating his breakfast, began to explore the lake shore in the hope of coming upon a deserted camp. To his great disappointment, however, though he met with traces of one, yet no food was discoverable, nor had his friends left any notice for him of their movements. All he found was a dinner-fork, which was of great use afterwards in digging roots, and a yeast powder tin, which he converted into a drinking cup and dinner pot. It never occurred to him that they might have cached food, which he learned afterwards they had done in several spots along their route. He left the place in deep dejection, and prepared to follow the trail of the party to the Madison.

As usual, he made a little bower for himself, that night, by the side of the fire.

He was aroused, however, from his peaceful slumbers, by the sensation of roasting flesh, which, if it had been any other than his own, might doubtless have been more pleasant. Starting up, he found his shelter and the adjoining forest in a broad sheet of flame. His left hand was badly hurt, and most of his hair singed off in escaping from the semicircle of burning trees, and, to crown these disasters, he lost his buckle-tongue knife, his pin fish-hook, and tape fish line.

He describes the scene very graphically. How marvellous it was to witness the flash-like rapidity with which the flames devoured the great tall pine, leaping madly from top to top, and lighting up with lurid gloom the surrounding scenery. "Roaring, cracking, crashing on it travelled, till it appeared as if the whole forest was alight, and the whole hillside an ocean of glowing and surging fiery billows. The atmosphere was filled with driving clouds of suffocating smoke, and a broad and blackened trail of spectral trunks shorn of limbs and foliage, was left to mark the immense sweep of the devastation."

He determined to give up what would most probably be a fruitless search for any trace of his companions' route, and selected for a landmark the lowest notch in the Madison Range.

He shall continue the narrative himself.

"Carefully surveying the jagged and broken surface over which I must travel to reach it, I left the lake and pushed forward into the midst of its intricacies. All the day I struggled over rugged hills, through windfalls, thickets, and matted forests, with the rock ribbed beacon constantly in view. As I advanced it receded, as if in mockery of my toil. Night overtook me with my journey half accomplished. The precaution of obtaining fire gave me warmth and sleep, and long before daylight I was on my way. The hope of finding an easy pass into the valley of the Madison, inspired me with fresh courage and determination, but long before I arrived at the base of the range, I scanned hopelessly its insurmountable difficulties.

It presented to my eager vision an endless succession of inaccessible peaks and precipices, rising thousands of feet sheer and bare above the plain."

He was seized with despair, his journey of the last two days had been in vain! He seated himself on a rock which commanded the valley, and gazed along the only route which now seemed possible—down the Yellowstone, through endless dreary miles of forest and mountain. If he could only find a pass, twenty miles at most would take him into the Madison Valley, and ten more restore him to food and friends! While he was trying to make up his mind he experienced a curious hallucination, which, as he says, turned out a merciful Providence in the end. An old clerical friend of whose opinion and advice he entertained a great regard, appeared standing before him, and charged him to go back instantly and without delay, as there was no food to be procured, and the idea of scaling the rocks was madness. He pleaded, in answer, that his shoes were worn out and his clothes in tatters, and he would rather make a last trial for a pass, or perish in the attempt. But his old friend was inexorable; insisted on his returning, and promised to accompany him back to the lake. "Overcome by these persuasions, I plodded my way over the route I had come. Whenever I was disposed to question the wisdom of this, my old friend appeared to be near with words of encouragement, but his reticence on other subjects both surprised and annoyed me. I was impressed at times, during the entire journey, with the belief that my return was a fatal error, and if my deliverance had failed, should have perished with the conviction."

He arrived once more at the Yellowstone Lake four days after leaving the Madison Range, hungry and worn out with travel, and almost abandoning all hope of escape.

However, he started on the trail down the river next day, determined to make this one last effort, and his sinking spirits were presently revived by the discovery of a fresh gull's wing lying on the ground—

the remains of some animal's meal. He made a fire on the spot, mashed the bones with a stone, and putting them into his tin pot, made a half-pint of excellent broth, a refreshing change from his thistle diet.

Gradually a sort of lethargic state seems to have come over him. He lost all consciousness of time, and, though he was almost starving, felt no sense of hunger.

He no longer suffered pain. The sores on his feet, the burn on his hip, and festering crevices at the roots of his fingers, ceased to give him the least concern.

He also describes his hours of slumber as being at this period most consolatory. He sat down to immense tables loaded with appetizing viands, and freely partook of all those dainties which his soul most loved. The whole night would be spent in getting up a sumptuous dinner— roasting, baking, boiling—and then in eating of it, " even to repletion ! " The awakening to the cold comfort of his thistle-roots must indeed have been bitter. We will let him describe his arrival at the Yellowstone Falls in his own words.

"It was a cold gloomy day when I arrived in the vicinity of the falls. The sky was overcast and the snow-capped peaks rose chilly and bleak through the biting atmosphere. The moaning of the wind through the pines, mingling with the sullen roar of the falls, was strangely in unison with my own saddened feelings. I had no heart to gaze upon a scene which a few weeks before had inspired me with rapture and awe. One moment of sunshine was of more value to me than all the marvels amid which I was famishing. But the sun had hid his face and denied me all hope of obtaining fire. The only alternative was to seek shelter in a thicket. I penetrated the forest a long distance before finding one that suited me. Breaking and crowding my way into the very midst, I cleared a spot large enough to recline upon, interlaced the surrounding brushwood, gathered the fallen foliage into a bed, and lay down with a prayer for sleep and forgetfulness. Alas! neither came. The coldness increased through the night. Constant friction with my hands, and unceasing beating with my legs and feet, saved me from freezing. It was the most terrible night of my journey, and when at the early dawn I pulled myself into a standing posture, it was to realize that my right arm was partially paralyzed, and my limbs so stiffened with cold as to be almost immovable. I literally dragged myself through the forest to the river. Seated near the verge of the great cañon below the falls, I anxiously awaited the appearance of the sun. That great luminary never looked so beautiful as when, a few minutes later, he emerged from the clouds, and exposed his glowing beams to the concentrating power of my lens. I kindled a mighty flame, fed it with every dry stick and broken tree top I could find, and without motion, almost without sense, remained beside it several hours. The great falls of the Yellowstone were roaring within three hundred yards, and the awful cañon yawned almost at my feet, but they had lost all charm for me. In fact, I regarded them as enemies, which had led me to destruction, and felt a sullen satisfaction in morbid indifference." Like the Ancient Mariner with waters all around him, and not a drop to drink, so our poor wanderer seems to have had his sufferings much aggravated by the good food abounding around him, but which he was unable to secure. He constantly passed herds of deer, elk and antelope; and the lakes and rivers teemed with ducks, geese, swans and pelicans. Trout also were plentiful; but, though he spent hours in trying to catch them with a hook fashioned from the rim of his broken spectacles, and with grasshoppers for bait, yet, he never succeeded in tasting that excellent fish. Once he found a small stream full of minnows, which he caught with his hands and ate raw. But they made him very sick, and were evidently affected by some mineral in the water, and rendered unwholesome.

He was so exhausted on reaching Tower Falls, that, finding a snug bear's den in a hollow tree, he could not resist creeping into it, first lighting a circle of logs around him, which happily kept away the rightful owner.

Then, on leaving the river and striking the open country, his only source of food seems to have failed him, and it was only by putting himself on to half rations, that the thistle roots, with which he had filled his pouches before leaving the forest, could be made to last for the several days of travel between him and Boteler's Ranch, his destination! One day, after building a huge fire, he found he had lost his lens, and had to retrace his steps five miles before he found it. He was half frozen and nearly buried in another storm of snow, and his fire was blown out. Frightful dreams prevented his resting even when asleep. He describes his shrunken arms, the skin clinging to the bones like wet parchment.

And yet he struggled on, feeling that if he paused for rest now he would collapse altogether and sink dying upon the path. The solemn conviction came over him that death was near, that he had done everything a man could do, and that as he was now in the broad trail his remains would be found, and his friends relieved of doubt as to his fate.

But at the last moment deliverance was at hand; we will leave him to describe this.

"Groping along the side of a hill, I became suddenly sensible of a sharp reflection, as of burnished steel. Looking up, through half-closed eyes, two rough but kindly faces met my gaze.

"'Are you Mr. Evarts?'

"'Yes. All that is left of him.'

"'We have come for you.'

"'Who sent you?'

"'Judge Lawrence and other friends.'

"'God bless him, and them, and you! I am saved!' and with these words, powerless of further effort, I fell forward into the arms of my preservers in a state of unconsciousness. I was saved. On the very brink of the river which divides the known from the unknown, strong arms snatched me from the final plunge, and kind ministrations wooed me back to life.

"Baronet and Prichette, my two preservers, by the usual appliances, soon restored me to consciousness, made a camp upon the spot, and while one went to Fort Ellis, a distance of seventy miles, to return with remedies to restore digestion, and an ambulance to convey me to that post, the other sat by my side and ministered to my necessities. In two days I was sufficiently recovered in strength to be moved twenty miles down the trail, to the cabin of some miners who were prospecting in that vicinity. From these men I received every possible attention. A good bed was provided, game was killed to make broth, and their best stores placed at my command. For four days, at a time when every day's labour was invaluable in their pursuit, they abandoned their work to aid in my restoration. Owing to the protracted inaction of the system and the long period which must transpire before Prichette's return with remedies, my friends had serious doubts of my recovery.

"The night after my arrival at the

cabin, while suffering the most excruciating agony, and thinking that I had been only saved to die among friends, a loud knock was heard at the cabin door. An old man in mountain costume entered—a hunter, whose life was spent upon the mountains. He listened to the story of my sufferings, and tears rapidly coursed each other down his rough weather-beaten face. But when he was told of my present necessity, brightening in a moment, he exclaimed:

"'Why, Lord bless you, if that is all, I have the very remedy you need. In two hours' time all shall be well with you.'

"He left the cabin, returning in a moment with a sack filled with the fat of a bear, which he had killed a few hours before. From this he rendered out a pint measure of oil. I drank the whole of it. It proved to be the needed remedy, and the next day, freed from pain, with appetite and digestion re-established, I felt that good food, and plenty of it, were only necessary for an early recovery."

And so we take leave of him, safely landed amongst his friends, and soon sufficiently restored to return to his home.

There is one wish of his with which we cannot sympathize, expressed in conclusion to his narrative, viz., that the Yellowstone may become "the abode of civilization and refinement," under which "more auspicious circumstances," he thinks he might be induced to visit it again.

No; even at the risk of being lost, of having to live on thistle-roots for a month, one could hardly desire the surpassing charm of this wild region should be destroyed. Refinement and civilization, alas!—or so-called refinement and civilization—are a dubious addition to the beauties of Nature, especially when she manifests herself in all her wonder and savage glory, as she does in this marvellous land. Already some of the stage-houses have assumed too "civilized" an air, though those who ride through can avoid any jars from these prosaic associations, by keeping off the trail. There is horrible talk, too, of a railway to the Falls, which brings a vision before us —wafted from Niagara—of tea-gardens and advertisement boards, and we involuntarily shudder!

For those, therefore, who would see the Yellowstone without these attractions, one can only say, see it at once. For who can tell how long it will be as it is, and as one yet hopes it may remain—unspoilt!

www.ingramcontent.com/pod-product-compliance
Lightning Source LLC
Chambersburg PA
CBHW020305170426
43202CB00008B/499